The
Marshall Plan

MILESTONES
IN MODERN
WORLD HISTORY

The Boer War

The Bolshevik
Revolution

The British
Industrial Revolution

The Chinese
Cultural Revolution

The Collapse of
the Soviet Union

The Congress of Vienna

The Cuban Revolution

D-Day and the
Liberation of France

The End of Apartheid
in South Africa

The Establishment
of the State of Israel

The French Revolution
and the Rise
of Napoleon

The Great Irish Famine

The Indian
Independence
Act of 1947

The Iranian Revolution

The Manhattan Project

The Marshall Plan

The Mexican
Revolution

The Treaty of Nanking

The Treaty of Versailles

The Universal
Declaration of
Human Rights

MILESTONES
IN **MODERN**
WORLD HISTORY

1600 · · · 1750 · · ·   · · · 1940 · · · 2000

The
Marshall Plan

G.S. PRENTZAS

CHELSEA HOUSE
An Infobase Learning Company

The Marshall Plan

Chelsea House
An imprint of Infobase Learning
132 West 31st Street
New York, NY 10001

Library of Congress Cataloging-in-Publication Data

Prentzas, G. S.
The Marshall Plan / G. S. Prentzas.
    p.   cm. — (Milestones in world history)
Includes bibliographical references and index.
ISBN 978-1-60413-460-5 (hardcover)
1. Marshall Plan—Juvenile literature. 2. Economic assistance, American—Europe—History—20th century—Juvenile literature. 3. Europe—Economic conditions—1945—Juvenile literature. I. Title. II. Series.

HC240.P68 2009
338.91'730409045—dc22   2010026904

Chelsea House books are available at special discounts when purchased in bulk quantities for businesses, associations, institutions, or sales promotions. Please call our Special Sales Department in New York at (212) 967-8800 or (800) 322-8755.

You can find Chelsea House on the World Wide Web at http://www.infobaselearning.com.

Text design by Erik Lindstrom
Cover design by Alicia Post
Composition by Keith Trego
Cover printed by Yurchak Printing, Landisville, Pa.
Book printed and bound by Yurchak Printing, Landisville, Pa.
Printed in the United States of America

This book is printed on acid-free paper.

All links and Web addresses were checked and verified to be correct at the time of publication. Because of the dynamic nature of the Web, some addresses and links may have changed since publication and may no longer be valid.

CONTENTS

A Helping Hand

On June 5, 1947, George Marshall arrived in Cambridge, Massachusetts, to accept an honorary degree from Harvard University. The university had chosen to honor the former U.S. Army chief of staff and current U.S. secretary of state for his key role in the Allied victory in World War II (1939–1945). While serving as the U.S. military's highest-ranking officer, Marshall had received widespread acclaim for his outstanding management of the United States' enormous war effort. *Time* magazine had named him their Man of the Year in 1943. Prime Minister Winston Churchill of Great Britain had praised Marshall's hard work, hailing him as the "organizer of the victory."[1]

Harvard had offered Marshall an honorary degree in 1945 and 1946. He had been unable to attend those ceremonies. Marshall, however, accepted the university's offer in 1947.

On June 5, 1947, Secretary of State George C. Marshall (*left*) receives an honorary degree of doctor of laws from Dr. Reginald Fitz of Harvard University. In his address at the university commencement, the former chief of staff of the Army outlined the European recovery program that would come to be known as the Marshall Plan.

Marshall believed that the ceremonies would be an ideal occasion for him to announce quietly a major foreign policy proposal. President Harry Truman had appointed Marshall secretary of state five months earlier. The U.S. secretary of state is the government official in charge of the nation's foreign policy. The most daunting task that Marshall faced in his new position was dealing with the economic, political, and human difficulties facing Europe in the aftermath of World War II.

A TERRIBLE TOLL

World War II began in September 1939 when Germany invaded neighboring Poland. Poland's allies France and the United Kingdom immediately declared war on Germany. The powerful German army easily invaded and occupied Belgium, Denmark, the Netherlands, Luxembourg, and France. It then began fighting against the United Kingdom and the Soviet Union. Most European countries and many nations around the world were eventually drawn into the conflict. One of Germany's allies, Japan, occupied much of Asia, including part of China and French Indochina (present-day Vietnam). A surprise attack by Japanese warplanes on Pearl Harbor, a U.S. naval base in Hawaii, in December 1941 brought the United States into the war. It joined the United Kingdom, the Soviet Union, and other Allied nations in the struggle against Germany, Japan, and other Axis nations.

Unlike most previous wars in Europe, World War II spread far beyond traditional battlefields. Warfare engulfed cities and civilian populations throughout Europe. German invasions and occupations ripped apart families, communities, and countries. The Germans demolished such major cities as Le Havre, France; Warsaw, Poland; and Kiev and Minsk in the Soviet Union. As Allied forces began to push back German forces in 1943, ground battles and intense Allied bombing campaigns destroyed many other European cities and towns. The German cities of Hamburg, Dresden, and Berlin were among those reduced to smoldering ruins. Allied forces captured Berlin, Germany's capital, on May 2, 1945, ending the war in Europe. (The war would continue in the Pacific theater until Japan surrendered three months later.)

Powerful new weapons—such as ballistic missiles, long-range bombers, and nuclear weapons—made the Second World War the most destructive war ever. The economic losses were astonishing. Warfare had demolished factories and other industrial facilities throughout Europe. More than half of housing in large cities had been destroyed. Thousands of bridges and countless miles of roads and railroad tracks had been ruined. Millions of acres of rich farmland were now wastelands, many pockmarked with bomb craters or dotted with unexploded landmines.

Six weeks before the German surrender, a *New York Times* reporter observed, "The human problem the war will leave behind has not yet been imagined, much less faced by anybody. There has never been such destruction, such disintegration of the structure of life."[2] The war's human toll was staggering. Between 1939 and 1945, nearly 37 million people died from war-related causes in Europe. (Estimates of the number of deaths caused by World War II worldwide range from 50 million to 70 million.) Nineteen million of the dead—more than half—were civilians. Several nations suffered massive casualties. Twenty percent of Poland's population died during the war. Other nations—Yugoslavia (12 percent), Soviet Union (9 percent), Greece (7 percent), and Germany (6.5 percent)—also experienced significant losses. After Allied troops captured Germany, the world was shocked to discover that the Nazis had systematically murdered about 6 million Jews because they supposedly threatened the "racial purity" of Germany. Many had been killed in work prisons, known as concentration camps.

At war's end, more than 13 million people were displaced from their homes or homelands. Nearly 20 million faced starvation. The war had shattered countless lives. Many survivors walked around in a daze. Jobs and food were scarce. Despair gripped the continent. There seemed to be little hope for the future.

In the immediate aftermath of the war, Europe began to recover very slowly. Europeans started rebuilding factories and reopening their businesses. Farmers planted new crops. In 1946, industrial production increased across the continent. Farmers and factories, however, still could not produce

World War II was the most destructive war in human history, with vast swaths of Europe suffering catastrophic damage. The aftermath of the battle for Isigny, France, is seen here, with the center of this little town in ruins on June 18, 1944. The Marshall Plan sought to help Europeans rebuild their continent.

enough goods to meet the needs of people. Almost all everyday items—such as flour, milk, clothing, and coal—were in short supply. Food shortages often meant skipped meals. Young people collected scrap wood and families burned their furniture for warmth.

The scarcity of products led to steep price increases. In France, for example, prices rose 80 percent during 1946. The increase in food prices affected everyone. In the summer of 1946, the United Nations estimated that as many as 100 million Europeans were malnourished. As that year drew to a close, Europe was still staggering when another calamity struck the continent.

The winter of 1946–1947 was the worst one that anyone in Europe could remember. Strong winds, bitterly cold temperatures, and record-breaking snowstorms paralyzed the United Kingdom. Snow accumulated as high as 20 feet (6 meters) in some places. On January 30, 1947, the Thames River froze over, halting coal shipments from northern England to London. Without coal, power stations were forced to shut down. People struggled to stay warm. Most of England's factories stayed closed for three weeks. On the continent, snowstorms and a deep freeze caused misery everywhere.

Still reeling from the brutal winter, Europeans suffered yet another blow when the long-awaited spring arrived. As the unusually deep snow packs melted, widespread flooding occurred, damaging towns, businesses, and farmlands. The summer of 1947 provided no relief. It was one of the hottest and driest summers on record. Crops withered from the heat and lack of rain. Farmers stopped sending their meager harvests to city markets. They hoarded food for their own families and grain for their livestock. In France, food shortages resulted in riots.

DARK HORIZONS

The natural disasters that struck Europe in 1947 left the continent teetering on the brink of collapse. In a speech the previous year, Churchill described the continent's troubles: "And what is the plight to which Europe has been reduced? . . . [O]ver wide areas a vast quivering mass of tormented, hungry, care-worn and bewildered human beings gape at the ruins of their cities and homes, and scan the dark horizons for the approach of some new peril, tyranny or terror."[3]

Because their factories could not produce enough goods to satisfy demand, Europeans bought large amounts of products and raw materials from the United States. American industries had remained untouched by the war, and the U.S. economy soared after the war. Having little to sell to the United States in return, Europe began to experience a serious trade imbalance. A "dollar gap" arose as European payments to the United States far exceeded U.S. payments to Europe. As a result, the value of the U.S. dollar increased, and the value of European currencies plunged.

By 1947, the threat of economic and financial collapse made many Europeans lose faith in their governments and currencies. It made communism—which promised economic stability, equality, and peace—more appealing. Even before the war, communism had been viewed by an increasing number of Europeans as an alternative to capitalism. The worldwide Great Depression of the 1930s had brought about widespread unemployment, misery, and dissatisfaction with European capitalism. During the war, communists and socialists had played key roles in resistance movements that fought against the Germans. In contrast, some large European companies and well-known wealthy families had been seen as collaborators because they conducted business with the Nazis.

After the war, support for communism gained momentum throughout Europe. Communist and socialist parties captured 40 percent of the vote in 1946 elections in Italy and Czechoslovakia. By 1947, membership in the French Communist Party swelled to nearly a million people. Both Greece and Yugoslavia seemed to be sliding into civil wars, with communist factions in each country appearing to have the upper hand.

The Truman administration became deeply concerned about the direction that Europe seemed to be heading. An economic collapse would harm the U.S. economy. The continued Soviet presence in postwar Germany and Eastern Europe particularly troubled U.S. government officials. Policymakers realized that the military victory had not been enough to safeguard democracy and free-market economies in Europe. The threat of communism and Soviet influence spreading beyond Eastern Europe and into Western Europe required prompt action. The administration considered a speedy European economic recovery and the preservation of democratic governments in Europe vital to the security and economic interests of the United States. Marshall's team began to formulate a plan to revive commerce and ensure future political stability in Europe.

A SOLDIER AND A STATESMAN

A graduate of Virginia Military Academy, George Catlett Marshall (1880-1959) accepted a commission as a U.S. Army lieutenant in 1902. He served in the Philippines and later helped plan major U.S. battles during World War I (1914-1918). Marshall rose steadily through the military ranks. He commanded junior officers, including Omar Bradley, Dwight Eisenhower, and George Patton, who would later serve as renowned generals during World War II.

On September 1, 1939, the same day that Germany invaded Poland, President Franklin D. Roosevelt appointed Marshall as the Army's chief of staff. He worked tirelessly to build up the United States' small, peacetime army. He transformed an army of 200,000 poorly trained, poorly equipped soldiers into the world's best-equipped military, numbering 8.3 million soldiers.

Once the United States entered World War II in 1941, Marshall quickly earned international acclaim for brilliantly managing U.S. armed forces in Europe and the Pacific. Marshall directed the planning for the massive Allied invasion of France in 1944. Roosevelt had wanted to assign him

FRIENDLY AID

On a beautiful late spring day in Cambridge, Marshall watched as Harvard handed out degrees to nearly 2,200 graduates. Because so many of its students delayed their studies to serve in the military during the war, the university had its first full-sized graduating class since 1941. Marshall was among a dozen distinguished guests, including physicist J. Robert Oppenheimer and poet T.S. Eliot, receiving honorary degrees that morning.

as the field commander for the D-Day operation but chose Eisenhower instead. As army chief of staff, Marshall had become indispensible to Roosevelt, who wanted him to remain in Washington.

On the day that Germany surrendered, Secretary of War Henry Stimson summoned Marshall and about a dozen other high-ranking officers to his office. Stimson told Marshall, "I have never seen a task of such magnitude performed by a man. . . . I have seen a great many soldiers in my lifetime and you, sir, are the finest soldier I have ever known."*

After the war, President Harry Truman appointed Marshall as secretary of state. In June 1948, Marshall suggested a plan that would eventually help save Europe from postwar economic collapse. That program, which became known as the Marshall Plan, earned the statesman the Nobel Peace Prize. Marshall was the first career soldier ever to win the award.

Shortly before Marshall died in 1959, the United Kingdom's former prime minster, Winston Churchill, called him "the last great American."**

* Greg Behrman, *The Most Noble Adventure* (New York: Free Press, 2007), p. 13.
** Leonard Mosley, *Marshall: Hero for Our Times* (New York: Hearst, 1982), p. 521.

In presenting Marshall with his honorary LL.D. (doctor of laws) degree, Harvard President James Conant paid tribute to Marshall as an "American to whom Freedom owes an enduring debt of gratitude, a soldier and statesman whose ability and character brook only one comparison in the history of this nation."[4] Conant was comparing Marshall to George Washington.

Marshall was scheduled to give a speech that afternoon at a meeting of the Harvard Alumni Association. After the other five speakers made their remarks, Marshall rose to speak. He prefaced his short speech by thanking Harvard officials: "I'm profoundly grateful and touched by the great distinction and honor and great compliment accorded me."[5]

The secretary of state then began his prepared remarks by calling attention to the seriousness of the economic and political situation in Europe. "I think one difficulty is that the problem is one of such enormous complexity that the very mass of facts presented to the public by press and radio make it exceedingly difficult for the man in the street to reach a clear appraisement of the situation," he stated. "Furthermore, the people of this country are distant from the troubled areas of the earth and it is hard for them to comprehend the plight and consequent reactions of the long-suffering peoples, and the effect of those reactions on their governments in connection with our efforts to promote peace in the world."[6]

Marshall continued, asserting that Europe's economic recovery "will require a much longer time and greater effort than had been foreseen."[7] He assessed what measures were needed and the consequences of inaction: "Europe's requirements for the next three or four years of foreign food and other essential products—principally from America—are so much greater than her present ability to pay that she must have substantial additional help or face economic, social, and political deterioration of a very grave character."[8]

Marshall then reached the most important passage of his speech. He proposed a new approach to help Europe get back on its feet:

The remedy lies in breaking the vicious circle [of the dollar gap] and restoring the confidence of the European people in the economic future of their own countries and of Europe as a whole. . . . It is logical that the United States should do whatever it is able to do to assist in the return of normal economic health in the world, without which there can be no political stability and no assured peace. Our policy is directed not against any country or doctrine but against hunger, poverty, desperation and chaos. Its purpose should be the revival of a working economy in the world so as to permit the emergence of political and social conditions in which free institutions can exist. Such assistance, I am convinced, must not be on a piecemeal basis as various crises develop. Any assistance that this Government may render in the future should provide a cure rather than [something that merely eases the symptoms of the problem]. Any government that is willing to assist in the task of recovery will find full co-operation I am sure, on the part of the United States Government.[9]

Marshall then added an important condition to any aid that the United States would provide to Europe. He asserted, "The initiative, I think, must come from Europe. The role of [the United States] should consist of friendly aid in the drafting of a European program and of later support of such a program so far as it may be practical for us to do so."[10]

He ended the historic speech by pointing out the importance of Europe's recovery to the United States:

It is virtually impossible at this distance merely by reading, or listening, or even seeing photographs or motion pictures, to grasp at all the real significance of the situation. And yet the whole world of the future hangs on a proper judgment. It hangs, I think, to a large extent on the realization of the American people, of just what are the various dominant factors. What are the reactions of the people?

What are the justifications of those reactions? What are the sufferings? What is needed? What can best be done? What must be done?[11]

In this speech, Marshall was suggesting that the European nations set up their own program for reconstruction. He indicated that the United States would be willing to provide financial aid to help Europe carry out that program. The speech provided no details about how this aid would be provided. It did, however, make it clear that Europeans would have to take responsibility for the recovery efforts. That European aid program that eventually resulted from Marshall's speech would become known as the Marshall Plan.

The Response to Marshall's Speech

Marshall's Harvard speech received little immediate attention in the American press. A few large newspapers published short articles mentioning the speech, but most news outlets ignored it. Marshall and the Truman administration were relieved that the speech went mostly unnoticed in the United States. Although delivered to an American audience, Marshall had directed his comments toward government leaders in Europe. Across the Atlantic Ocean, his speech had an immediate impact.

THE WESTERN EUROPEAN ALLIES

On the night of June 5, 1947, Foreign Secretary Ernest Bevin of Great Britain sat in bed listening to "American Commentary," a weekly British Broadcasting Corporation (BBC) radio program focused on U.S. politics and culture. He was surprised when the program began broadcasting a speech by George Marshall. A day earlier, the U.S. State Department had released a draft copy of the secretary of state's speech to several influential European journalists. After reading the speech, BBC reporter Leonard Miall had persuaded the home office in London to let him recite it on the June 5 "American Commentary" program. (Bevin later admitted he thought that he was hearing an actual live broadcast of Marshall delivering his speech at Harvard.)

As Bevin listened to Marshall's speech, he immediately realized its importance. Europe had just emerged from a dreadful winter, which had brought the continent's first modest steps toward postwar economic recovery to a near standstill. With their economic systems nearly shattered, most European governments were desperate for assistance. Bevin later observed that, at the time, he viewed Marshall's idea of creating a broad, new European recovery plan as a "lifeline to a sinking man. It seemed to bring hope where there was none."[1]

The next morning, Bevin spoke with other British government officials. They responded positively to Bevin's description of the speech. He immediately called Foreign Minister Georges Bidault of France. Bevin suggested that the two men meet to discuss Marshall's speech. He wanted the United Kingdom and France to draft a coordinated response to the American proposal. Bidault agreed, and they made plans to meet in Paris.

Bidault and other French government officials welcomed the news of Marshall's proposal. Inflation, labor strikes, and the dollar gap were battering France's weak economy. The growing success of Communist Party candidates in French elections had unsettled the government of Prime Minister Paul Ramadier and created political turmoil. Unlike the British, however, French officials were not wholeheartedly enthusiastic about Marshall's proposal. They were concerned about the effect that American aid would have on the status of Germany. France was fiercely opposed to having its longtime rival rapidly reintegrated into postwar Europe. They wanted financial reparations from Germany to help pay for the extensive damages to France caused by the German invasion and occupation. French officials sought to ensure their country's future security by insisting that Germany not be allowed to rearm itself. They also worried that the Soviet Union would react negatively to the American offer. If the French government found itself taking sides against the Soviets on the issue of the proposed American aid program to Europe, the French Communist Party might cause more problems, such as calling for labor strikes.

In other European countries, Marshall's proposal received mostly positive, but mixed, reviews. Government officials and citizens recognized the benefits that an American-funded aid program could provide. The consensus was that unless they received help, European nations would collapse. Everyone knew that the United States was the only country with enough resources to provide the needed assistance. Many Europeans worried, however, that the aid would come with too many strings attached. They did not expect the Americans to provide assistance without wanting something in return.

Marshall's speech had not mentioned Germany, so it was unclear whether the still-divided nation would be included in the proposed recovery plan. Negotiations on how to rebuild Germany's economic and political systems were stalled, and there seemed to be no way out of the deadlock. The prospect of an American aid program, however, thrilled leaders in Germany's three western occupied zones, which were controlled by the United States, the United Kingdom, and France. Leaders in the fourth zone, controlled by the Soviet Union, remained silent on Marshall's speech.

THE SOVIET RESPONSE

The Soviet Union's ambassador to the United States, Nikolai Novikov, sent his initial assessment of Marshall's speech to Soviet officials in Moscow. He wrote that the European aid

Foreign Secretary Ernest Bevin of Great Britain (*left*) greets Vyacheslav Molotov, his Soviet counterpart, at the opening of the Four-Power Foreign Ministers Conference on Germany and Austria in London, England, on November 25, 1947. Though the Soviet Union had been asked to join the proposed European recovery plan, Soviet leader Joseph Stalin sought to disrupt the Marshall Plan to forestall American influence in Europe.

program envisioned by Marshall had two goals. First, it would try to prevent the economies of Western Europe from collapsing. Second—and more vital to Soviet interests—Novikov believed that the program would serve as a way for the United States to mold Western Europe into a unified federation of nations. The Americans could use this alliance to frustrate Soviet foreign policy goals. Soviet officials interpreted Marshall's proposal as a plot to control Western Europe and threaten the Soviet Union's security. An article in a major Soviet newspaper, *Pravda Ukraine*, provided insight into the Soviets' view. It described Marshall's proposal as "a plan for political pressures with dollars and a program for interference in the internal affairs of other states."[2]

REACTION IN THE UNITED STATES

The response to Marshall's speech in the United States was sluggish. The lead story in major American newspapers on the day following the speech reported President Truman's remarks about recent events in Hungary. Communists had seized control of that country's government while Prime Minister Ferenc Nagy was out of the country. The June 6 edition of the *New York Times* carried a short article that provided an account of the initial response to Marshall's speech—in Paris. In his article, "France is Stirred by Marshall Plan," reporter Harold Callender was the first person to use the phrase "Marshall Plan" to describe the proposed European recovery program. Most American newspapers, however, ignored Marshall's speech. They had little to report to their readers because Marshall's speech contained few details. It seemed like another impractical idea to be added to the long list of proposed government programs that would never be put into action.

Marshall first discussed the proposed European recovery plan at a news conference a week after his speech. He told reporters that he was sending Undersecretary of State Will Clayton to Europe to meet with European leaders. A successful businessman and skilled diplomat, Clayton had been an early supporter of providing economic aid to help Europe recover from the war. Marshall emphasized to reporters that Clayton would not be presenting a U.S. plan to Europe. Instead, he would be there only to listen. European leaders would be the ones to form a plan to help their nations rebuild. Many Americans doubted that the Europeans could cooperate with one another to create this program. A workable plan emerging from Europe seemed unlikely.

At the time, Marshall's proposal was out of step with popular opinion in the United States. The nation had spent a huge amount of money (more than $300 billion) and resources during World War II. More than 300,000 of its soldiers had been killed. The war effort had required Americans to make a lot of sacrifices. Rationing programs for gasoline, meat, sugar, and other common goods had affected everyone's daily life.

Now that the war was over, many Americans felt that it was time for their government to spend its money at home. Although they had sympathy for the suffering of Europeans and were willing to lend a helping hand, Americans were primarily concerned about getting their lives back to normal. Many worried about their own country's economy. Business and industry had expanded greatly during the war, but the postwar economic outlook was troubling. Inflation was on the rise. Soldiers had returned from the war only to find that many jobs offered low wages. They joined other workers in labor strikes demanding better pay. Many Americans still recalled the dark days of the prewar Great Depression. They did not want to return to the misery of those times.

These sentiments had played a role in the shift of power in national politics. In the 1946 elections, Republicans gained control of both the U.S. Senate and House of Representatives. The party's candidates had won by promising lower taxes and reduced government spending, including significant cuts in defense and foreign aid budgets. The Republican Congress became a roadblock for many of the proposals made by the Democratic president's administration.

Any legislation authorizing money for a European recovery program would have to pass through the powerful Senate Foreign Relations Committee. Its new chairman, Arthur Vandenberg of Michigan, publicly supported Marshall's idea. The Republican senator, however, was unsure whether the

United States could afford to foot the bill. He felt that many voters would prefer that the federal government spend money on domestic programs rather than on foreign aid. In a letter to the director of the American Association for the United Nations, Vandenberg noted: "I certainly do not take it for granted that American public opinion is ready for any such burdens as would be involved."[3]

In anticipation of a recovery aid plan being created by Europeans, the White House and the State Department began preparing for the expected legislative battle with the Republican Congress. One White House adviser suggested that the program be called the Truman Plan. Truman, however, insisted that it be called the Marshall Plan. He wanted Marshall's key role in developing the idea to be recognized. Truman also worried that congressional Republicans would reject any proposed bill with his name attached to it. Marshall's prestige as a soldier and statesman would be a valuable asset in getting any legislation passed.

THE CONFERENCE OF EUROPEAN NATIONS

When Ernest Bevin and Georges Bidault met in Paris on June 17, they agreed that their two countries must seize the opportunity that George Marshall had offered. They discussed the next steps that needed to be taken. European nations should hold a conference to draft a plan to guide the reconstruction under Marshall's proposed recovery program. The conference should also create committees to coordinate agriculture, industrial production, and other important economic sectors throughout Europe.

Bevin and Bidault agreed that the Soviet Union should be asked to participate in the recovery program. The two men invited the Soviets to attend a planning meeting that would take place before the larger conference. The Soviets agreed to meet with Bevin and Bidault to discuss the proposed recovery plan. On June 27, Foreign Minister Vyacheslav Molotov of

The overt Soviet influence on Eastern Europe, especially in the areas it controlled of Germany, were on immediate display in the postwar period. Seen here, Lieutenant Edith A. Waldhaus, Lieutenant Claudette Forand, and Captain Helen A. Lyons, nurses with the 113th Evacuation Hospital in Berlin, look at the portrait of Stalin on the Unter den Linden in Berlin, in 1945. In the background is the ruin of the Adlon Hotel.

the Soviet Union met with his British and French counterparts. Soviet leader Joseph Stalin had instructed Molotov that he should not agree to any plan that required conditions for nations receiving the economic aid.

At their meeting with Molotov, Bevin and Bidault insisted that the aid program had to require economic cooperation among European nations. Molotov firmly insisted on a simple program that would distribute aid without requiring cooperation or any other condition. The meeting became deadlocked as both sides refused to budge. The United States separately announced that Germany would be eligible for aid under the proposed recovery program. When Bevin and Bidault told Molotov that they agreed with the Americans, Molotov informed them that the Soviet Union would not participate in the Marshall Plan. He walked out of the meeting.

On July 4, 1947, Bevin and Bidault invited 22 European nations to participate in a conference to create a plan for European recovery. Since their meeting with Molotov, British and French officials had drafted a broad plan of action. Europe would first help itself by establishing programs for economic cooperation. The nations would then repeal laws and other barriers that restricted trade between each other. Once this was accomplished, Europe would request financial aid and other needed resources from United States. To avoid delays, Bevin and Bidault set a tight deadline. The final plan and first cooperative actions would be completed by September 1. Europe would then present the final recovery plan to U.S. officials.

Bevin and Bidault had extended invitations to the Soviet Union and seven Eastern European countries—Albania, Bulgaria, Czechoslovakia, Hungary, Poland, Romania, and Yugoslavia—that were under its influence. After their failed meeting with Molotov, the two men knew that the Soviets would not accept but wanted to force the Soviets to decline the invitation publicly. U.S. officials were hopeful that the aid promised by the Marshall Plan would help lure some of the Eastern European countries away from the Soviet Union.

The Conference for European Nations, as the planning conference became known, was scheduled to begin on July 12, 1947. One week earlier, Soviet officials informed their foreign ambassadors throughout Eastern Europe that the Soviet Union would not participate in the conference. Soviet officials, however, wanted them to urge the leaders of Eastern

European governments to accept the offer and then sabotage the plan. The idea was that representatives of these countries could disrupt the conference by disagreeing with proposals, introducing counterproposals, and using delaying tactics.

FORGING AN AGREEMENT

On the morning of July 12, 1947, delegates from 16 European nations gathered in an elegant conference room at the Foreign Ministry building in Paris. They came together to forge a joint European recovery plan. They would present this plan to the United States, whose secretary of state, George Marshall, had proposed an aid program to help Europe rebuild. Noticeably missing from the conference were representatives from the Soviet Union and Eastern European countries, which had declined to participate in the Marshall Plan.

As the delegates began to decide the initial organizational details—such as schedules, committees, and agendas—it became clear that it would be difficult to resolve issues caused by conflicting national interests. Delegates disagreed on nearly everything. In any discussion or negotiation, they tried to secure any advantage that they could for their own country—or block other countries from gaining any benefit. They tried to meet in private with American officials to promote their own aid needs. Seemingly, the only thing that the delegates agreed about was that they all needed American aid.

In order to draft a feasible plan to submit to the Americans, each nation agreed to supply an honest estimate of how much aid it needed. All of them submitted estimates that greatly exaggerated their needs. "Everybody

These countries would eventually withdraw their delegates from the conference. The Soviets hoped that this discord would fracture the conference and that other nations would also withdraw.

---

cheated," confided a Dutch delegate.* The total amount of the estimates far exceeded any aid budget that U.S. officials would approve.

Two groups with markedly different concepts of the proposed aid program eventually emerged. One faction viewed the Marshall Plan as an opportunity to finance large, long-range building projects, such as oil refineries. France was the leading member of this group. The other faction saw the proposed aid program as an effort to assist Europe with short-term recovery projects. The aid would keep European economies functioning and help return their factories, farms, and other businesses to their prewar levels of production. The United Kingdom and the Netherlands were among the members of this group.

As the September 30 deadline for drafting a final plan neared, the two groups finally came together. A U.S. promise of interim aid motivated the countries to come to an agreement. Delegates finally agreed that their nations needed to make concessions in order to create an integrated plan for European recovery. They committed their countries to establishing an organization to set production levels for certain goods, such as steel and coal, for each country. They also agreed to start negotiating reductions in trade barriers between each other. Delegates presented their joint aid proposal to American officials on September 23, 1947.

---

* Philip C. Brooks, "Oral History Interview with E.H. van der Beugel, June 1, 1964." http://www.trumanlibrary.org/oralhist/beugel.htm.

The Eastern European governments were pleased to accept the invitation to the conference. Several were interested in receiving aid and hoped that they could overcome Soviet resistance. On July 7, all seven Eastern European countries sent messages to the United Kingdom and France accepting their invitation to the conference. Soviet officials, however, abruptly changed their minds and ordered their ambassadors to discourage the seven governments from attending the conference. Crushed by the change in the Soviets' position, six of the countries immediately withdrew their acceptances.

Czechoslovakia, however, still wanted to attend the conference despite the Soviet opposition. Stalin immediately summoned Czech officials to meet with him in Moscow. He pressured them not to attend the conference and promised that the Soviets would send aid to Czechoslovakia. (This aid program, which created an economic union between the Soviet Union and Eastern Europe to help rebuild those countries, would be known as the Molotov Plan.) The Czech leaders reluctantly agreed to withdraw their acceptance. Foreign Minister Jan Masaryk of Czechoslovakia later lamented, "I went to Moscow as the foreign minister of an independent sovereign state. I returned as a lackey of the Soviet Government."[4]

Fourteen nations accepted invitations to the conference. In addition to the United Kingdom and France, Austria, Belgium, Denmark, Greece, Iceland, Ireland, Italy, Luxembourg, the Netherlands, Norway, Portugal, Sweden, Switzerland, and Turkey agreed to send delegations to the conference. The seven Eastern European nations—Albania, Bulgaria, Czechoslovakia, Hungary, Poland, Romania, and Yugoslavia—joined the Soviet Union in declining to attend. (Although it wanted to join in the aid program, officials in Finland also decided not to attend the conference. Their country's vulnerable location next door to the Soviet Union made Finnish leaders cautious about upsetting the Soviets.) The decisions about attending the conference had made the divisions in Europe clear. Western European nations attending the conference were either aligned with the United States or officially neutral. Eastern European nations turning down the invitation were aligned with the Soviet Union.

When the Paris conference began on July 12, 1947, the delegates faced an overwhelming task. They had six weeks to create a broad plan to help the continent's economy recover. Getting 16 countries to agree on this plan seemed impossible. The countries had different cultures, distinct economic and political circumstances, and conflicting interests and needs. With the British and French delegations leading the way, however, the delegates set up committees to handle various tasks. Representatives from every country sat on each committee. One committee focused on organizing the conference. Technical committees were formed to handle issues involving key economic sections, such as agriculture and transportation. The key committee, known as the Committee of European Economic Cooperation (CEEC), began working to establish the broad ideas and rules that would guide cooperation among the 16 nations. The CEEC finished drawing up its final proposal for the European recovery. It formally presented the proposal to the U.S. government on September 23, 1947.

Speaking for the Conference delegates, Ernest Bevin emphasized that Europe was not asking for charity from the United States. The European nations that wanted to participate in the Marshall Plan were willing to surrender some of their national sovereignty for the common good of Europe. They had agreed to work together to cooperate on economic matters, such as reducing trade barriers among themselves. They had agreed to make all the sacrifices necessary to quicken the recovery of their nations. Bevin told reporters, "Here is our report. It is now for the American people and the American Congress to decide whether this program . . . should be fulfilled and whether Europe can by this means contribute to the peace and prosperity of the world."[5]

The Economic
Recovery Program

Nearly every European nation except the Soviet Union and its Eastern European allies joined together to seek aid from the United States under the Marshall Plan. Finland declined to participate because of its proximity to the Soviet Union. Spain had not been invited to take part because the facist dictatorship of Francisco Franco held power in Spain. Still under Allied occupation in 1947, Germany had not yet established an independent government. (West Germany would join the Marshall Plan two years later.) Once presented with the proposed recovery plan by the CEEC, the Truman administration began to draft legislation to create funding for the Marshall Plan. Its most difficult task would be to convince Congress to enact the legislation.

DRAFTING THE MARSHALL PLAN

When drafting legislation to propose to Congress, policymakers in the Truman administration wanted the Marshall Plan to achieve three key goals. First and foremost, they wanted to stabilize the economies of U.S. allies in Western Europe. Second, they sought to create larger markets for U.S. goods and services. An economically sound Europe could afford to import more American products, thereby strengthening the U.S. economy. Third, the administration wanted to make sure that the United States would not be drawn into a third world war. It worried that the economic and political turmoil in Europe could lead to another armed conflict. The increasing popularity and success of communist parties in Western European countries—as well as the threats posed by the Soviet Union's growing strength in Europe—unsettled most Americans.

State Department employees worked many late nights drafting the Marshall Plan legislation. They analyzed stacks of economic data from each participating country. They assessed many different theories that proposed ways to strengthen the European economy. In addition to preparing the technical details of the recovery program, they wanted to create a reasonable legislative package that Congress would enact. As policymakers drafted the proposed legislation, they made an effort to keep the proposed costs as low as possible and to include a time limit. They hoped to assure skeptical lawmakers, particularly Republicans, that the Marshall Plan would not be an expensive and open-ended commitment for the United States. They also wanted to emphasize that this recovery program was different than previous aid packages. Under the Marshall Plan, European nations would agree to increase economic cooperation among themselves. They would develop their own recovery plans and programs. Marshall Plan funds would not be another foreign-aid handout. They would provide aid to help Europeans help themselves.

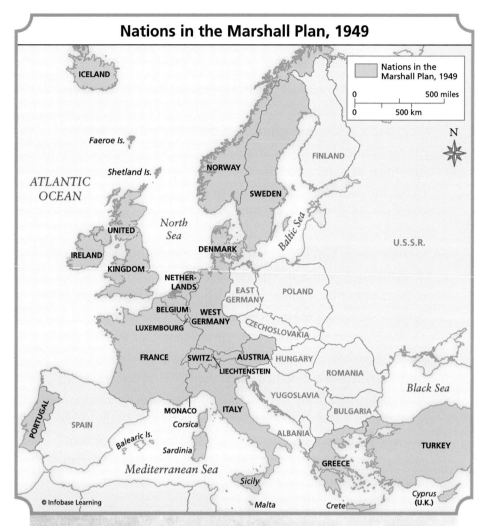

Nations in the Marshall Plan, 1949

Nations in the Marshall Plan, 1949

This map highlights the nations that benefited from the Marshall Plan. An American program of economic aid designed to stimulate European growth after World War II, the Marshall Plan was informed by an awareness that the punitive measures of the Treaty of Versailles following World War I had contributed to the rise of Nazi Germany.

PERSUADING CONGRESS AND THE PUBLIC

Members of Congress quickly realized the importance of the Marshall Plan legislation being drafted by the Truman administration. Many members of Congress decided to take a first-hand look at the economic and political situation in Europe. In late August 1947, a group of 18 congressmen set out to visit Europe. They spent 45 days on the continent, visiting almost every country. More than 200 additional members of Congress also went on their own fact-finding tours to Europe. After assessing the conditions in Europe, many members of Congress concluded that European recovery would require a large amount of American aid.

The congressional trips to Europe increased the number of Marshall Plan supporters in Congress. Support for European aid, however, had begun to decline among the American public at large. Several members of Congress informed the Truman administration that, despite their personal support for the goals of the Marshall Plan, they would have to consider the mood of voters in their districts when casting their votes. Realizing that a significant shift in public opinion would jeopardize their plans, the administration arranged a public relations campaign to bolster public support for the Marshall Plan.

President Truman called for a national program to conserve food. He explained that these efforts would allow surplus food supplies to be sent to hungry, malnourished people in Europe. A volunteer effort called the Friendship Train was organized. A freight train traveled around the country to collect food supplies from donors. The donations would be sent to Europe as a gift from American citizens. Civic organizations, restaurants, and other groups made large donations of basic foodstuffs, such as sugar and flour, to the Friendship Train. Shipping companies offered to transport the food shipments across the Atlantic for free.

Marshall Plan supporters outside of the U.S. government formed a lobbying organization. Known as the Committee for the Marshall Plan, its mission was to provide the American public with information about the Marshall Plan. Headed by Henry Stimson, a former secretary of war, the organization brought together influential Americans, including newspaper

The thirty-third president of the United States, Harry S. Truman served from 1945 to 1953. After ascending to the presidency following Franklin D. Roosevelt's death, Truman authorized the atomic bombing of Japan in the closing days of World War II and the implementation of the Marshall Plan to aid the rebuilding of Europe.

editors, university scholars, and business and labor leaders. The committee raised money from donors, hired a full-time staff, and sought volunteers. It started a petition drive to collect at least a million citizens' signatures in support of the Marshall Plan. The committee would present the petition to Congress. It bought advertisements, sent out news releases, and sponsored educational lectures around the country. The committee also published brochures that answered frequently asked questions about the Marshall Plan. Behind the scenes, it lined up crucial support from labor unions, religious groups, and other civic organizations.

A CRISIS IN FRANCE AND ITALY

While the Truman administration was at work drafting the Marshall Plan legislation and trying to increase support for it in Congress and with the American public, the political situation in Europe worsened. In response to the Marshall Plan, the Soviet Union created the Communist Information Bureau (Cominform) in September 1947. The organization's unspoken mission was to enable the Soviets to exert more control over the plans and activities of national communist parties throughout Europe. One of Cominform's major goals was to counteract the Marshall Plan and economic cooperation among Western European nations. Soviet spokesman Andrei Zhdanov alleged that the Marshall Plan was part of a larger U.S. strategy of "world domination."[1] He declared that the United States was using economic aid merely as part of its plan for "enslaving Europe," ensuring that its governments would comply with American demands.[2] He pledged, "The U.S.S.R. will put all effort into seeing that the Marshall Plan is not realized."[3]

One of Cominform's first directives was to support the disruption of the French and Italian governments. The communist parties in France and Italy enjoyed strong support among laborers and labor unions. In October 1947, the French and Italian communists called for national labor strikes. To turn public sentiment against the French and Italian governments, they also instigated deadly clashes with police. To make the governments look ineffective, operatives sabotaged transportation and other public facilities. The French and Italian economies ground to a standstill. Rumors of armed conflict and communist takeovers echoed throughout Western Europe. Some Americans opposed to the Marshall Plan began asking publicly why the United States should even bother with a recovery plan if communists were going to seize control of Europe.

In response to the growing troubles in France and Italy, President Truman requested a special session of Congress. He wanted Congress to pass a temporary aid bill to provide support for France and Italy. The aid would help shore up the wobbly French and Italian governments until Congress could enact the Marshall Plan legislation. In a November 17 speech to a special session of Congress, Truman urged Congress to pass an interim aid package immediately. He asserted that "the future of free nations in Europe hangs in the balance."[4] He also asked lawmakers to fund the Marshall Plan, which his administration would soon present to Congress.

Administration officials testified before congressional committees in support of the interim aid package. The efforts to get the interim aid bill passed turned out to be a dress rehearsal for the Marshall Plan legislation. Many of the same arguments for and against the Marshall Plan were aired during consideration of the interim aid bill. In a speech to the Ohio Society of New York, Senator Robert Taft of Ohio voiced the reservations of many of his fellow Republicans. He pointed out that the previous European aid programs had failed. He asserted that the burden on U.S. taxpayers would be enormous. The aid program would likely lead to rationing, wage freezes, and inflation. He asked: "How far shall we make a present to other peoples of the fruits of our labors? Do the advantages to be gained in foreign policy outweigh the disadvantages at home?"[5]

On September 23, 1947, Walter Kirkwood is photographed after landing in New York City, following his trip to Paris, France. He is holding one of five sacks, each containing a 230-page report of the needs of 16 European nations seeking Marshall Plan aid. The Europeans asked for almost $16 billion in U.S. credits for the years 1948 to 1951.

Despite these concerns, Congress passed a bill authorizing $522 million in temporary aid for France and Italy on December 15, 1947. Only six members of Congress voted against it. Even Taft ultimately voted for the aid package. Although the bill authorized significantly less money than the administration had requested, White House and State Department officials were relieved. At least Congress had appropriated some emergency funds.

News that the Americans would be providing interim aid provided immediate relief to desperate government officials in France and Italy. It gave them funds for relief programs and provided a message of hope for their citizens. Meanwhile, communists undermined their own cause. In France, communist operatives tore up a section of railroad tracks, which caused a passenger train to derail. They thought that the train would be carrying police. It was instead carrying regular passengers. Sixteen people died, and many more were injured. Public sentiment quickly turned against the French Communist Party. Labor unions fractured, splitting into anti-communist and pro-communists factions. Many French workers ended their strikes and returned to work. Dockworkers returning to their jobs volunteered to work for free to unload the first Friendship Train food shipments, which were just arriving at the port of Le Havre. Only a few weeks earlier, the workers had been protesting against the United States meddling in European politics. Now, they were pitching in to assist an American aid project.

PASSAGE OF THE MARSHALL PLAN

During the month of January 1948, more than 100 government officials and experts testified before the Senate Foreign Relations Committee and the House Foreign Affairs Committee. Nearly 100 others submitted written reports. One of the reports weighed more than 3 pounds (1.36 kilograms). Witnesses supporting and opposing the Marshall Plan speculated on its potential economic and political impact. Economist Calvin Hoover cautioned, "[T]he goods which we furnish Europe must come out of our own potential standard of living and not out of some mythical surplus."[6] Will Clayton warned that "if Western Europe is overrun by communism, . . . the economic consequences of such a disaster would be very, very, very great to us. We would have to reorder and readjust our whole economy in this country if we lost the European market."[7]

The most influential person to testify before Congress was George Marshall. In his testimony before the Senate committee, he emphasized the importance of the legislation:

> So long as hunger, poverty, desperation, and resulting chaos threaten the great concentration of people in Western Europe, there will steadily develop social unease and political confusion so widespread, and hope of the future so shattered that the historic base of western civilization . . . will take on a new form in the image of the tyranny that we fought to destroy in Germany. . . . We shall live, in effect, in an armed camp, regulated and controlled. . . . There is no doubt in my mind that the whole world hangs in the balance.[8]

Because the Marshall Plan was so large and touched on so many issues, it enabled the Truman administration to respond effectively to whatever concerns members of Congress had. If a congressman was worried about the spread of communism, the administration showed how the plan would thwart communist objectives in Western Europe. If a congressman complained that the plan would be too expensive, the administration sent him a report showing the potential cost of losing European markets. Supporters of the Marshall Plan used many lines of reasoning to advocate passage of the legislation. It provided a way to defeat communists in France and Italy. It would help contain Soviet expansion and lessen their power and influence.

(continues on page 44)

GEORGE MARSHALL'S CONGRESSIONAL TESTIMONY

When considering legislation, the U.S. Senate and the House of Representatives often conduct hearings to gain insight into issues relevant to the proposed bill. On January 12, 1948, Secretary of State George Marshall testified at a hearing before the Committee on Foreign Affairs in the House of Representatives. He discussed the need for—and the many benefits of—the Marshall Plan:

> The European recovery program necessarily must be considered in relation to the foreign policy of the United States, which in its simplest form is concerned with those conditions abroad which affect or could later affect the future security and the well being of our Nation.
>
> What we desire . . . is a stable, cooperative, and confident world. But such a world does not exist today. We must deal with the existing situation in our effort to promote peace and security. The situation in Europe has not yet developed to the point where the grim progression from economic uncertainty to tyranny is probable. But without United States support of European self-help, this progression may well become inevitable. Therefore, it is proposed that our Nation . . . assist in setting in motion the processes of recovery in the second most productive area in the world. The aid suggested is designed to prevent the economic strangulation which now threatens western Europe and through that vital area endangers the free people of the world. This aid must cure the illness without impairing the integrity of the nations we wish to support. The challenge of our task is great.

We are faced with the necessity of making a historic decision. The proposed program will impose burdens upon the American people, but the quantity of exports contemplated is less than those of the past 15 months. The decision should be made on the basis of our most fundamental interests and I submit that none of these are more compelling than enduring peace and individual freedom.

Europe must be restored if a durable peace is to be attained. The United States has expended vast resources in the quest for peace. If by the expenditure of an additional amount, . . . we can finish the job, certainly we should do so in our own interest as well as that of the world at large.

. . . I know you are aware of the momentous importance to the world of your decisions. While we are dealing at the moment with the drab though vital facts of economic life, they carry with them fateful consequences. The automatic success of the program cannot be guaranteed. The imponderables are many. The risks are real. They are, however, risks which have been carefully calculated, and I believe the chances of success are good. There is convincing evidence that the peoples of western Europe want to preserve their free society and the heritage we share with them. To make that choice conclusive they need our assistance. It is in the American tradition to help. In helping them we will be helping ourselves— because in the larger sense our national interests coincide with those of a free and prosperous Europe.*

---

* "Marshall Testimony of January 12, 1948, United States Foreign Policy for a Post-War Recovery Program Hearings Before the Committee on Foreign Affairs, House of Representatives, Eightieth Congress, First and Second Sessions," Washington, D.C.: Government Printing Office.

(continued from page 41)
It would help avoid another world war. It would help reduce military spending. It would provide funds to rebuild Germany. It would increase U.S. exports to Europe. It would prevent another economic depression.

All of these arguments began to sway reluctant congressmen. The administration also succeeded in convincing the American public that the Marshall Plan was necessary. A public opinion poll revealed that the economic and political arguments being made in Washington had swayed many Americans. Most people who supported the Marshall Plan considered it to be a humanitarian effort.

It soon became clear to opponents of the Marshall Plan that the Truman administration had gained enough support in Congress to pass the legislation. They began to focus on the changes that they could make to the administration's draft legislation. A small group of congressmen joined together to weaken the Marshall Plan. Led by Taft and Representative Christian Herter of Massachusetts, these legislators sought to reduce the Marshall Plan's budget, limiting the plan's appropriation to $4 billion a year. They also proposed that Congress review and authorize the budget for each of the three remaining years.

To prevent a reduced budget from gaining additional support in Congress, Senator Arthur Vandenberg stepped in. He asked the White House to change its proposed budget. Instead of asking for the entire amount—$18 billion over four years—at once, he suggested that the administration ask for $5.6 billion the first year and allow Congress to renew funding thereafter. Vandenberg promised that he could get the votes needed to approve the initial $5.6 billion appropriation. He also pledged that he would make sure that Congress renewed the budget in the future.

On February 13, the Senate Foreign Relations Committee approved the administration's bill by a 13–0 vote. They sent the bill to the full Senate for consideration. On March 14, the

Senate voted 69–17 in favor of the bill. The Senate bill provided $5.3 billion for the first year of a four-year program.

As the House of Representatives considered the legislation, events in Europe helped ensure that the Marshall Plan would be enacted. On March 17, Truman again addressed Congress. Three weeks earlier, communists had seized control of the government of Czechoslovakia. The only remaining member of the government who had not joined the communists, Foreign Minister Jan Masaryk, was found dead on the pavement beneath the open window of his office. His death was deemed a suicide, but it was unclear whether he had taken his own life or had been assassinated. Truman told Congress, "The tragic death of the Republic of Czechoslovakia has sent a shock-wave through the civilized world. . . . There are times in world history when it is far wiser to act than to hesitate."[9] Newspaper stories about the coup—as well as editorials pondering whether war was near—fanned fears of communist takeovers and the Soviet menace to Europe.

Two days later, the House Appropriations Committee approved the bill and sent it to the full House. The committee's report recommended that the House pass the bill to turn back communism in Europe. On March 30, the House of Representatives voted 329–74 to authorize a $6.2 billion foreign aid package. It provided $5.3 billion for European aid through the Marshall Plan. The additional $900 million was allotted for aid to Greece, Turkey, and China and for an international emergency relief program for children.

On April 3, 1948, President Truman signed the Foreign Assistance Act of 1948 into law. At the signing ceremony, Truman said, "This measure is America's answer to the free world." George Marshall was not present for the signing. He was traveling to a diplomatic conference in South America. He would later say, "It was just a struggle from start to finish, and that's what I'm proudest of, that we actually . . . put it over."[10]

The Aid Begins

The Foreign Assistance Act provided funds for the Marshall Plan, officially known as the European Recovery Plan (ERP). Unlike most previous aid given to Europe, these funds would not be handouts. Rather than giving cash to the Marshall Plan countries, the United States would provide aid in the form of goods and services. The ERP would buy these goods and services—almost all of them from American companies—and ship the goods (or supply the services) to people and companies in Europe.

ORGANIZING THE ERP

To manage the funding and to supervise the recovery projects of the ERP, the Foreign Assistance Act created a federal agency, the Economic Cooperation Administration (ECA). It would be responsible for carrying out a complicated and highly visible government program. Over the next four years, it would be in charge of spending a $17 billion budget on aid projects. (In current dollars, it would be about $150 billion). That amounted to about 2 percent of the entire U.S. government budget for those four years.

The Truman administration wanted to appoint an ECA administrator as quickly as possible. White House officials had several prominent Democrats in mind to lead the agency. Senator Vandenberg, however, stepped in. He firmly suggested that the White House appoint someone whom the Republicans in Congress would find acceptable. The senator recommended Paul Hoffman, a well-known businessman. As president of the Studebaker automobile company, he had pulled the company out of bankruptcy. He had also founded the Committee for Economic Development (CED), a nonprofit organization of prominent business leaders that promoted economic growth. Through his work with the CED, Hoffman had been one of the foremost Republicans supporting the Marshall Plan. Hoffman had impressed Congress with his testimony before the Senate Foreign Relations Committee on the potential economic impact of the Marshall Plan. White House officials agreed with Vandenberg. Truman appointed Hoffman as administrator of the ECA. He was sworn in on April 9, 1948.

Working out of his hotel room in Washington, D.C., Hoffman immediately jumped into his daunting assignment. He began building the ECA from scratch. He hired the best and brightest people from business, government, and universities to staff the agency. Hoffman focused his efforts on managing the ECA and promoting the Marshall Plan. He would travel widely, giving speeches and meeting with government officials in the United States and Europe. A major part of his job was to trumpet the Truman administration's vision of the ERP. He wanted to make sure that Congress, the American public, and European allies would continue to support the Marshall Plan.

The American ambassador to France, Jefferson Caffery, addresses an assembly during a ceremony at the harbor of Bordeaux, France, on May 10, 1948. The celebration marked the arrival of the *John H. Quick* as the first ship bringing aid to France under the Marshall Plan.

Hoffman's first hire was Richard Bissell, an economics professor at the Massachusetts Institute of Technology (MIT). Bissell was a noted expert on building national economies. After reviewing the first group of aid requests from Europe, Bissell quickly authorized $35 million in ERP aid. All of the early aid requests asked the ECA to send specific items, particularly food, fuel, and farm and factory machinery.

The very first Marshall Plan shipment left from Galveston, Texas, on April 17. The freighter *John H. Quick* set out for

Europe, carrying more than 20 million pounds (9 million kg) of grain. Over the next few weeks, more American ships, transporting items including seeds, fertilizer, tractors, and oil, headed across the Atlantic to deliver aid under the Marshall Plan. Austria, the United Kingdom, France, Greece, Italy, and the Netherlands were among the first nations to receive the first shipments of Marshall Plan aid.

Bissell developed procedures to approve aid requests and to spend Marshall aid funds. He started an innovative program known as counterpart funds. Under this program, the ECA used Marshall Plan funds to buy ECA-approved goods and services from American businesses and ship them to Europe. European consumers used their own currencies to buy U.S. goods and services. For example, if the Italian government requested a shipment of fertilizer to improve agricultural productivity, the ECA would review the request. If the ECA approved the request, it would buy fertilizer from an American company and ship it to Italy. When an Italian farmer needed fertilizer, he would buy it from a local business using lira (Italy's currency). The business would then deposit the money in the Italian government's central bank. These deposits were the counterparts of the Marshall Plan's funds that the ECA had used to buy the fertilizer from the American company. The ECA worked with Italian officials to identify the best way to spend the counterpart funds that amassed in the central bank.

Marshall Plan countries used their counterpart funds to reduce their national debts—that is, they repaid the loans that they had taken out to operate their governments. They also used the counterpart funds to make loans to companies to rebuild or update their factories. The counterpart fund program helped keep traditional European economies working. It allowed consumers and businesses to pay for what they received.

Within three months, Hoffman had hired more than 400 employees to staff the ECA. Building the agency had been easier than he had anticipated. "It started with the Marshall speech," Hoffman recalled. "The concept was a noble one. The people in the organization wanted to work for something worthwhile. . . . You couldn't want a better motivation that that."[1] Resisting pressure from the White House to make political appointments, Hoffman hired the best person he could find for each position.

The ECA moved into an office building near the White House. It also set up offices in Europe. Hoffman convinced Averell Harriman to head up the ECA's European branch, known as the Office of the Special Representative (OSR). Harriman, a successful businessman and respected diplomat, had previously served as the U.S. ambassador to the Soviet Union and as the U.S. ambassador to the United Kingdom. He oversaw the OSR office in Paris and the ERP mission offices. An ERP mission office, run by a mission chief, was set up in each of the 16 Marshall Plan countries.

Because the situation in Europe was so dismal in the spring and summer of 1948, food, medicine, and similar relief supplies made up a large part of early Marshall Plan aid. ECA and European government officials hoped that this humanitarian aid would help improve workers' health and productivity. ECA ships arriving in European ports received rousing welcomes. Some of the aid projects achieved immediate success. For example, when a large U.S. shipment of carbon black—a chemical used to make tires, rubber, ink, and other products—arrived in Birmingham, England, the Dunlop Rubber Company reopened the world's largest tire plant. Tens of thousands of employees soon returned to work at the factory. The Marshall Plan also had an important emotional impact by providing Europeans with hope. They began to believe that their countries could rebuild from the war. They began to trust that their governments could be effective.

By the end of June, the ECA had approved recovery-aid requests totaling nearly $750 million. About three-quarters of this aid had gone to the United Kingdom, France, and Italy—

the countries with the largest populations and economies. About one-third of the monies had been spent on food, feed, and fertilizer. The remaining amount had been used to buy raw materials, machinery, and other products. About 15 percent had been spent on shipping the goods to Europe. Overall, the ERP had paid for nearly half of all the U.S. goods imported by Marshall Plan countries during the first six months of 1948.

THE FIGHT AGAINST COMMUNISM

The Marshall Plan also had a major political impact during its early months. The April elections in Italy had emerged as a critical early test of the impact of the Marshall Plan. Communists had won about 40 percent of the vote in a previous election. U.S. officials worried about the consequences if they were able to win enough seats to gain control of the Italian government. State Department official George Kennan observed that the United States' "whole position in the Mediterranean, and possibly in Western Europe, would probably be undermined" if the Italian Communist Party won the election.[2]

The U.S. government used various methods to support Italy's ruling party, the Christian Democrats. The U.S. Postal Service organized an effort called "Freedom Flights." It gathered individual aid packages being sent from Italian Americans to relatives in Italy. The Postal Service then express shipped them to Italy by airplane. The Friendship Train program gathered donations to send to Italy. The U.S. government sponsored radio broadcasts supporting democracy. It also secretly gave at least a million dollars to Italy's various noncommunist parties. All of these efforts began to pay off. Large groups of Italian workers became embittered with all the strikes instigated by the communists. Alarmed by the coup in Czechoslovakia, even Pope Pius IX spoke out against the communists. The Truman administration applied additional pressure by announcing that if the communists gained control of the government, Italy would not receive Marshall Plan aid.

Both the Christian Democrats and the Communist Party portrayed the election as voting for the United States or for the Soviet Union. The election gave Italian voters a clear choice. A vote for the Christian Democrats (or other noncommunist parties) was a vote for alliance with the United States and the Marshall Plan. A vote for the Italian Communist Party was a vote against American interference and imperialism. On election day, April 18, 1948, 94 percent of Italy's 26 million voters voted. The Christian Democrats and their allies won nearly 49 percent of vote. The Communist Party and its allies received

THE COLD WAR

The Cold War (1947-1991) was a period of heightened tensions between nations that dominated world politics and public attention for most of the second half of the twentieth century. Major events during the Cold War included the Berlin Blockade (1948), the Korean War (1950-1953), the Vietnam War (1954-1975), the Cuban Missile Crisis (1962), the construction (1961) and demolition (1989) of the Berlin Wall, and the collapse of the Soviet Union (1991).

The Cold War began when the relationship between the United States and the Soviet Union soured after World War II. The Soviet Union had joined with the United Kingdom, France, and other countries to defeat Germany. The political differences between communism (in the Soviet Union and its allies) and democracy (in the United States and its allies), however, created a sharp division between the former allies. To protect itself from future invasions, the Soviet Union took steps to gain firm control of the Eastern European nations that bordered it. It installed obedient communist governments in these countries. The United

31 percent. The Christian Democrats' victory strengthened the United States' position in the region. For communists in Italy and throughout Western Europe, it was a deflating loss.

During the spring of 1948, the Soviet Union launched a propaganda campaign against the Marshall Plan. Hoffman had once noted that the ultimate goal of the Marshall Plan was "to stop the spread of communism."[3] The Soviets and communist leaders in Western Europe were ready for a war of words. They called the Marshall Plan "an instrument of preparation of war."[4] The propaganda project fell flat, however, as Marshall

States and its allies began to fear that communism would threaten their national interests by spreading to other countries around the world.

For the next 40-plus years, the relationship between the Soviet Union and the United States fluctuated between periods of open aggression and phases of eased tensions and diplomatic compromise. Both the United States and the Soviet Union possessed nuclear weapons. As a result, each side was reluctant to fight each other directly. A "hot" war between the two countries could destroy them. The battle-grounds of their "cold" war included lining up allies (either by persuasion or through political, economic, or military pressure), massive military build-ups, espionage, propaganda campaigns, and clashing positions in the United Nations and other international organizations. The conflict also played out in wars between other nations. In the Korean War, the Vietnam War, and the Soviet invasion of Afghanistan—and in other conflicts around the world—the United States and the Soviet Union inevitably backed opposing sides.

The Cold War ended in 1991 when the Soviet Union's economy and political unity fell apart. The Soviet Union then split into 15 separate nations.

Plan aid began arriving in Europe. The loss in the Italian election, coupled with the fatal derailment of the passenger train in France by communist operatives, swung public opinion away from communism and the Soviet Union. Joseph Stalin saw that his plan to spread Soviet influence over Western Europe was slipping away. As a result, the Soviets turned their attention away from Western Europe to a prize that was within their reach: Berlin.

THE BERLIN AIRLIFT

At the end of World War II, the victorious Allies had divided Germany—and its capital city, Berlin—into four occupation zones. In early 1948, the United Kingdom, France, and the United States began to merge their three zones in western Germany. They planned to create an independent, democratic nation. The Soviet Union controlled the fourth zone, eastern Germany. Soviet officials strongly opposed a united Germany because their country had suffered greatly during the German invasions of World War I and World War II.

On June 24, 1948, to foil progress toward reunification and to gain control of all of Berlin, the Soviet Union cut off all land and rail routes into West Berlin. (The three zones of Berlin controlled by the United Kingdom, France, and the United States made up West Berlin.) West Berlin was located about 100 miles (161 km) inside the Soviet occupation zone. It had a population of about 2.5 million people who depended entirely on shipments from the western zones of Germany for all of their food and other supplies. The Berlin Blockade, as the Soviet maneuver became known, prevented these shipments. Lucius Clay, the military governor of Germany's U.S. zone, called the blockade "one of the most ruthless efforts in modern times to use mass starvation for political coercion."[5]

The United States, the United Kingdom, and France responded to the Soviet blockade by launching a massive airlift effort. On July 1, airplanes began delivering food and other

During the Berlin Blockade, the only way for West Berliners to receive aid from western Germany was via airlifts. Seen here, in October 1948, children gaze hopefully at the sky, waiting for candy bars to be dropped from a C-54 Skymaster passing overhead on its approach to Tempelhof Airport during the airlift.

necessities to West Berlin. The airlift transported about 5,000 tons (4,536 metric tons) of supplies each day. The Soviets had hoped that the blockade would undermine the prestige of the British, French, and Americans in Germany. Their plan backfired. It spurred the Allies to establish an independent West Germany more quickly. It also led to the creation of a powerful United States–Western Europe military alliance, known as the North Atlantic Treaty Organization (NATO). NATO's mission was to defend Western Europe against Soviet aggression. The Soviets would eventually lift the Berlin Blockade in May 1949. More than 280,000 flights were flown during the Berlin airlift.

THE OEEC

While U.S. and Western European leaders dealt with the Berlin crisis, Paul Hoffman made sure that the ECA stuck to its original mission. During the first few months of the Marshall Plan, the ECA had focused its efforts on providing immediate humanitarian aid. Hoffman believed that the Marshall Plan countries now needed to take charge of their own economic recovery. "The idea," Hoffman observed, "is to get Europe on its feet and off our back."[6]

Reducing the dollar gap was a key element in European recovery. Marshall Plan funds could provide some assistance. To reduce the amount of their own money spent on U.S. imports, Europeans needed to increase their agricultural and industrial output. Two things would help to increase production: creating a common market among themselves and improving productivity. By integrating their economies as much as possible, European nations could enlarge the market for the products they made. Instead of relying on government tariffs and other trade restrictions to protect them, European companies would have to compete with businesses in the other Marshall Plan nations. To compete, they would have to increase worker productivity and lower their production costs.

To receive aid, the Marshall Plan countries had agreed to move toward greater economic integration. To help foster cooperation on economic matters, they created the Organization for European Economic Cooperation (OEEC). Based in Paris and headed by French economist Robert Marjolin, the OEEC was Western Europe's sister agency to the ECA. Its broad mission was to promote cooperation and economic integration between the 16 Marshall Plan nations.

OSR chief Averell Harriman met frequently with the OEEC's executive committee. He emphasized that, through the OEEC, the nations must draft a plan for how ERP aid would be distributed. He wanted to avoid having each of the 16 countries approach the ECA on its own, seeking to broker a deal just for itself. That would place too much burden on the ECA. More importantly, the countries would end up trying to undermine each other in order to get more aid for themselves. Harriman wondered whether the OEEC would be able to agree on anything. Western European countries had little history of cooperating. They had vastly different economies, political concerns, and aid needs. Harriman found himself constantly negotiating with OEEC officials. He kept nudging them toward creating a mutual recovery plan to present to the ECA.

In the summer of 1948, the Marshall Plan countries submitted their aid requests to the OEEC. ECA officials were not surprised to discover that the total amount of the requests far exceeded the ERP aid funds available. The bickering countries were unable to come to an agreement. Many countries did not want to expose their economic programs to the scrutiny of other countries. Behind the scenes, Harriman kept negotiating with representatives of each nation. Finally, in September, the deadlock was broken. Sensing that the U.S. government officials had become frustrated, the Marshall Plan countries became worried that the United States might withdraw aid altogether. OEEC representatives began to admit that they had a shared economic destiny. After hundreds of hours of negotiations, they were able to agree on aid request totals for each country.

On October 16, 1948, the OEEC delivered the plan for the Marshall Plan nations' economic program to Harriman. He told OEEC officials:

[T]here were those who said the task laid upon you was impossible. It was foolhardy, they held, to expect so many separate political entities to agree among themselves upon a cooperative program including the division of American aid and the reconciliation of the intricacies of each one's economic needs. . . . I rejoice with you in having a report that proves it can be done.[7]

THE IMPACT OF EARLY MARSHALL AID

By the time that the OEEC delivered its aid plan, the initial impact of the Marshall Plan had become clear. ERP humanitarian aid, together with a successful growing season in Europe, had increased the supply of food and eased hunger and malnutrition. From April to September, the total output of factories and mines in Marshall Plan countries had increased by 10 percent over the same period in 1947. In fact, the output had almost reached prewar levels.

In six months, the ECA had been built up. American and European public opinion strongly supported the Marshall Plan. A group of 16 European countries had overcome self-interest to begin a new era of economic cooperation. The successes of the Marshall Plan had undermined Soviet goals in Western Europe. In a report to Congress, the ECA affirmed that much progress had been made. There was still a great deal of work to be done, but Western Europe was beginning to recover and rebuild.

Recovery and Cooperation

After its first six months, the ECA started to shift its primary focus away from humanitarian aid and toward the kind of economic aid that the Marshall Plan had been created to provide. At any one time, as many as 150 freighters were crisscrossing the Atlantic Ocean loaded with goods purchased with Marshall Plan funds. In the United States, the ECA bought goods for approved projects from companies and arranged their shipment. In Europe, the government distributed these goods to businesses and consumers to help rebuild Europe's economy.

REBUILDING ECONOMIES

ERP shipments began to provide supplies that were essential to Europe's economic recovery. Most of these essential supplies were raw materials, which European companies used to make finished goods. Dockworkers at European ports noticed a change in the ERP cargo arriving from the United States. Instead of crates of grain, orange juice, and powdered milk, the ships were now carrying a dizzying assortment of raw materials. Dockworkers unloaded shipments of coal, petroleum, and other fuels, which helped reduce shortages until European coal mines and oil refineries returned to full production. They unloaded shipments of metals, such as copper and zinc, and chemicals, such as sulfur and borax, which kept factories operating and workers employed. They unloaded shipments of cotton, wool, and other fabrics, which allowed textile mills to keep making clothes and other goods. They unloaded tractors and machinery parts, which were scarce throughout Europe and much needed by farms and factories.

Thousands of Europeans—factory workers, farmers, and bakers—came into contact with goods supplied by the Marshall Plan every day. Each shipment of ERP-provided goods was embossed with the Marshall Plan symbol: a red, white, and blue shield with the slogan "For European Recovery: Supplied by the United States of America."

ERP assistance for the first year made up about 5 percent of combined national incomes of Marshall Plan nations. Because it consisted mostly of essential goods, the aid provided much more economic value than its original cost. ERP goods enabled businesses and entire industries to operate. For example, a load of cotton bought for $10,000 by the ECA in the United States could keep a French textile mill running. The mill could produce clothing that would be sold in local stores. The factory's owners and workers, the store's owners and workers, and consumers would all benefit. In addition, the mill's payment for the cotton would be deposited in France's counterpart fund account. The French government could use this money to rebuild or modernize its infrastructure—a country's basic facilities, such as power, transportation, and communication systems. Economists call this process a "multiplier effect." Each

One of the major investments of the Marshall Plan was in European infrastructure. Seen here is the André Blondel hydroelectric power plant on the Rhone River in France under construction in 1951. The plant was funded in large part by the Marshall Plan for the rebuilding of Europe.

dollar of aid led to more economic activity, thereby multiplying the original value of the aid.

Marshall Plan countries used counterpart funds for a variety of infrastructure projects. The Italian government began restoring railroads and building bridges. The French government began building dams to produce electricity, installing electrical lines, and updating the technology in its coal mines. Denmark modernized its steel mills. The Netherlands created additional farmlands through land-reclamation projects.

Greece began a training program to teach olive-farm workers new skills so that they could get better-paying jobs.

The ECA also began approving reconstruction projects. For example, Italian automaker Fiat asked for ERP funds to build a plant because its management wanted to develop and produce a new car model. The ECA agreed to fund the project if the Italian government and the automaker agreed to certain conditions. The Italian government had to start a major road-building program and eliminate its tax on gasoline. Fiat had to agree that its new model would be small and inexpensive. The ECA felt that Italy's economy would be boosted by an improved road system and wider car ownership and usage. ERP aid also helped bring about a unique cooperative project. A French shipbuilder manufactured ferries using steel from the United Kingdom and Denmark. It hired experts from the Netherlands to test the vessels before they were put into operation. ERP aid provided two large, American-made cranes that were needed to build the ferries.

ERP aid also funded many rebuilding projects in Greece. The country had suffered extensive damage during World War II. When German, Italian, and Bulgarian forces retreated in October 1944, they destroyed bridges, railroads, and shipping facilities. Allied bombing campaigns against the retreating troops damaged almost everything else. One U.S. official called Greece the "most thoroughly destroyed, disorganized, and demoralized country in Europe."[1] The most celebrated Marshall Plan project in Greece was the restoration of the Corinth Canal. To prevent the advancing Allies from using the shipping artery, the Germans had blocked the canal by using explosives to cause massive landslides on each of its ends. Various wreckage and debris—sunken ships, locomotives, and railway cars—also clogged the waterway. Clearing the canal was a daunting project. The Greek government lacked the money and machinery to do the job. The local ECA mission worked with Greek officials to bring in U.S.

In this photo, a train crosses the railway over Greece's Corinth Canal, which was cleared out, widened, and rebuilt thanks to the financial subsidies of the Marshall Plan. The canal, which reopened to shipping in 1950, was of strategic interest for crossing the isthmus.

contractors to clean up the mess. The Corinth Canal would be reopened to shipping traffic in 1950, just five years after the end of the war.

The ECA kept Congress informed of the ERP's progress through reports submitted every three months. In its June 1949 report, the ECA stated that "it was unmistakably evident that the flow of U.S. dollars and the efforts of the countries themselves had been effective in restoring the vitality of Western Europe. The importance to the U.S. and the world of a revived faith in the future cannot be overemphasized."[2]

To receive ERP funds, each Marshall Plan country had prepared a recovery plan and submitted it to the OEEC. The OEEC would then work with each country to approve projects in their plan. Once approved by the OEEC, the aid request was passed along to the ECA officials. If the ECA approved the project, it bought the necessary goods from suppliers and shipped them across the Atlantic. The ECA bought most ERP goods from American suppliers. Business and government leaders in Europe did not fail to notice the large increase in U.S. exports to Europe. They saw that American businesses, as well as the U.S. economy, were benefitting from the Marshall Plan. The ECA, however, also received complaints from all sides. European companies grumbled that American tariffs and trade barriers were preventing them from exporting their goods to the United States. U.S. companies began to pressure the ECA to buy finished goods. They worried that the ECA, by sending raw materials to Europe, was giving European companies a competitive advantage. They argued that American workers would lose their jobs if European workers started making more finished goods for the European market.

SELLING THE MARSHALL PLAN

Public relations played a vital role in the Marshall Plan. When Congress began considering the aid program in 1948, publicity efforts by the Committee for the Marshall Plan and other organizations helped convince legislators to pass the European Recovery Program bill.

Once Congress authorized the Marshall Plan, the ECA made sure that the Marshall Plan remained popular with politicians and the general public in the United States and in Europe. ECA Administrator Paul Hoffman gave many speeches and met with political and business leaders to shore up support for the ERP.

As a condition for receiving aid, Marshall Plan countries had agreed to publicize ERP aid projects. They held celebrations to

MARSHALL PLAN FILMS

After the ECA set up a movie production office in Paris, its management hired European filmmakers to produce films that would enhance the image of the Marshall Plan in Europe. Between 1948 and 1951, the movie office financed at least 280 short films, which were shown in theaters and other venues in Marshall Plan countries. The 20-minute (or shorter) films were recorded in 13 languages and touched on a range of topics. For example, *ERP in Action, No. 5* depicted Marshall Plan success stories, such as Greek sponge fishermen receiving diving equipment and the official launch of a Swedish oil tanker. *The Extraordinary Adventures of a Quart of Milk* took an unexpected comedic turn when an ERP-provided can of dehydrated milk spoke up, cutting off the film's boring narrator to tell its own story. *Me and Mr. Marshall* focused on Hans Fischer, a coal miner living in Germany's American zone. As the film showed scenes of destruction in the Ruhr region where Fischer lived, the 26-year-old wondered whether "Europe might just go kaput."* He concluded that the Marshall Plan was the best alternative to "uniforms and slogans and violence and barbed wire."** It would enable Germany to rebuild its farms and factories. Emphasizing the self-help aspect of the Marshall Plan, the film ended with this dialogue: "Name? Hans [Fischer]. Profession? Just call me a Marshall Planner."*** These films helped inspire Europeans to embrace the Marshall Plan, allowing American aid to help Europe help itself.

---

* Quoted in Roger Cohen, "Democracy as a Brand: Wooing Hearts, European or Muslim," *New York Times*, October 16, 2004.
** Ibid.
*** Ibid.

welcome freighters that delivered Marshall Plan shipments to their ports. They sponsored radio programs, lectures, and exhibits. They produced and screened films showing Marshall Plan successes. The governments were doing more than merely giving credit to the United States. They were emphasizing the need for increased worker productivity and economic growth. They were also counteracting communist propaganda that tried to make Marshall Plan aid appear to be a threat to European sovereignty and peace. The public relations campaign showed voters that their governments were using Marshall Plan aid to improve lives across Europe.

BUILDING GREATER UNITY

As ERP economic aid began to improve industrial and agricultural production, the United States began to shift the emphasis of the Marshall Plan once again. While the ECA worked with the OEEC on rebuilding and recovery projects, the Truman administration wanted to steer the Marshall Plan countries toward greater unity. The 16 nations had started meeting the production goals that they had agreed to when joining the EPR. They had made little progress, however, on their integration goals.

U.S. officials began pressing European officials to build a larger, more vibrant economy. They emphasized that the structure of Western Europe's economy needed to be changed in order to provide growth and stability in the future. U.S. officials believed that the Marshall Plan countries need to do two things: merge their economies and resolve the status of occupied Germany. U.S. officials realized that both of these requirements seemed difficult to achieve. Delay was no longer an option.

American policymakers asserted that the Marshall Plan countries needed to build a single large market. To do that, they needed to eliminate import quotas, tariffs, and other trade barriers. If Western Europe returned to its prewar economic structure, none of the individual nations' small independent

A worker clears rubble in the streets of West Berlin, Germany, under a Marshall Plan sign, in 1948. Marshall Plan aid to Germany enabled that country to rise from the ashes of defeat and helped make it one of the key economic engines of modern Europe.

markets would grow. Low productivity and high prices would be the result.

By merging their economies, the Marshall Plan countries would encourage companies throughout Western Europe to compete with each other. Business would have to modernize, innovate, and specialize to compete. Competition would improve productivity and economic growth. By creating a joint market, the Marshall Plan countries would not have to rely on U.S. imports. They could eliminate the dollar gap and create an economy that would provide prosperity and sustain itself. U.S. officials envisioned a Western European economy that would adopt some features of the U.S. economy, including a large, open market with few restrictions on trade.

Soon enough the nations' representatives found themselves, as one policymaker reported, "moving away from the original problem of how to organize a sensible aid program to the larger emphasis on the reorganization and the restructuring of the European economy and European society."[3] In their meetings with OEEC representatives and other Western European officials, the ECA began advocating greater economic unity.

The United States wanted the United Kingdom to take the lead on negotiations to solve the economic integration and status of Germany issues. The British government, however, began to oppose greater unity. British officials saw little reason to integrate their economy into Western Europe's. Despite the damage inflicted by the war, the United Kingdom still had the continent's largest economy. Government leaders wanted their country to maintain its political independence. The United Kingdom also had a much closer relationship with the United States than any of the other Marshall Plan countries. British officials believed that they could negotiate an even closer economic relationship with the United States.

ECA chief Paul Hoffman made several visits to Europe, meeting with heads of state, business leaders, labor leaders, and Averell Harriman and other OSR officials. On October 31, 1949, he addressed OEEC officials in Paris. Hoffman began his speech by congratulating them for making so much progress. He then asserted that the Marshall Plan countries now needed to "move ahead on a far-reaching program to build in Western Europe a more dynamic expanding economy which will promise steady improvement in the conditions of life for its entire people. This means nothing less than an integration of the Western European economy."[4] He further stunned the audience by implying that Congress would not renew ERP funds unless Western European governments started to integrate their economies.

Hoffman's speech—and his threat—had an immediate impact. On November 2, 1949, the OEEC announced its support for "a single large market in Europe."[5] It asked Marshall Plan nations to reduce their import quotas by at least 50 percent.

CURRENCY REFORM

By the time Hoffman gave his speech in Paris, the Marshall Plan countries had taken their first major step toward economic integration. In the early days of the Marshall Plan, the ECA had created a program to ease the exchange of national currencies between the 16 countries. Marshall Plan aid was used to finance the anticipated trade deficits of Marshall Plan countries. When one country's imports from another country amounted to less than its exports to that country, the ECA would make up the difference. This program helped countries avoid currency gaps within Europe. (This was similar to the dollar gap that the Western European countries had experienced because of their greater imports from the United States.) For example, if Greece's imports from Italy were greater than its exports to Italy, the ECA would provide aid funds to Greece to prevent its currency, the drachma, from losing too much value against the Italian lira. This program helped the countries maintain the value of their own currencies. It also eased the movement of imports and exports between countries and reduced the need for constant currency exchange.

The OEEC drafted a plan to create a new Western European agency to perform a similar role. On September 19, 1949, the Marshall Plan nations signed a treaty establishing the European Payments Union (EPU). The EPU agreement allowed trade between Marshall Plan nations to be made in any of their currencies. By keeping an accounting of imports and exports, the EPU could offset trade imbalances. The EPU was an immediate success. Within six months of its founding, trade between the Marshall Plan countries increased by an amazing 55 percent. About $500 million of Marshall Plan funds were used to set up and operate the EPU. ECA official Richard Bissell called the EPU "the greatest achievement of the Marshall Plan."[6]

The Marshall
Plan Ends

I n April 1950, the Marshall Plan entered its third year of operation. The ECA continued to administer the aid program, working closely with the OEEC and European governments. With the Cold War heating up, however, the European Recovery Program became less important. U.S. foreign policy began shifting away from providing economic aid and toward distributing military aid. The previous year, Congress had passed the Mutual Defense Assistance Act, which authorized $1.3 billion for military aid. Most of the weapons and other military hardware went to Marshall Plan nations. A conflict on the opposite side of the globe would have an even greater impact on the Marshall Plan.

THE KOREAN WAR

When Japan surrendered at the end of World War II, the United States and the Soviet Union took control of the Japanese territory of Korea. (Korea had signed a treaty in 1910, forfeiting its independence to Japan.) In August 1945, the two allies agreed to divide the Korean peninsula at 38 degrees north latitude, popularly known as the 38th parallel. The division would make the task of supervising the departure of Japanese troops from Korea easier. The Soviets would oversee the withdrawal north of the 38th parallel. The United States would oversee the withdrawal south of that line.

As Cold War tensions between the United States and the Soviet Union grew after the war, the temporary division of Korea soon became permanent. Separate governments emerged on each side of the divide. In 1948, communist leaders of North Korea refused to participate in an election being held in South Korea. Kim Il Sung was selected as prime minister of the Democratic People's Republic of Korea, or North Korea. Educated in the Soviet Union, Kim had gained fame for leading guerrilla attacks against the Japanese occupiers of Korea. The Soviet Union and China backed the new communist regime. In the south, voters elected Syngman Rhee as president of the Republic of Korea, or South Korea. Educated in the United States, Rhee had been a major figure in Korea's independence movement during the period of Japanese rule. The United States supported the new democracy.

The Kim and Rhee governments each claimed that it was the only lawful government of all of Korea, and each side declared that it wanted to reunify the country. Both sides amassed troops at the 38th parallel to protect their border. Both sides received military aid and equipment from their powerful supporters. The Soviet Union supplied North Korea with tanks, fighter planes, and other military equipment. Likewise, the United States helped arm and train South Korea. Both sides appeared to be about equal in strength. An uneasy stalemate ensued at the 38th parallel.

YOU ARE NOW CROSSING 38TH PARALLEL US CO.B 728MP

UN transport vehicles cross the 38th Parallel as they withdraw from Pyongyang, the North Korean capital, during the Korean War. The Korean conflict would help speed the end of the Marshall Plan.

On the morning of June 25, 1949, fighting broke out along the border. It was unclear who had fired the first shot, but it quickly became obvious which side was more powerful. About 75,000 North Korean troops burst through the South Korean defenses. The more experienced and better trained soldiers advanced southward. Many of South Korea's inexperienced soldiers abandoned their positions. Three days later, North Korean troops captured Seoul, the capital of South Korea.

President Truman felt that it was necessary to make a stand in Korea against further communist expansion in Asia, especially since China had become a communist nation in 1949, following the communists' victory in the Chinese Civil War. The United States immediately requested an emergency session

Seen here, everyday Koreans leave in a mass exodus from battle areas in North Korea during the Korean War. The war would last from 1950 to 1953 and end with the division of the Korean peninsula into the nations of North Korea and South Korea.

of the United Nations Security Council, which approved an international military response to the invasion of South Korea. It authorized U.N. forces to push North Korean troops back to the 38th parallel. The Soviet Union, a permanent member of the Security Council, boycotted the vote. The first American soldiers arrived in South Korea on June 30. Australia, Canada, the United Kingdom, and Turkey would later send some troops to Korea to fight alongside the Americans and South Koreans.

During the first year of the war, North Korean troops were able to drive U.N. forces into a corner of South Korea. On

September 15, 1950, however, U.N. troops made a daring land-ing behind North Korean lines. Led by U.S. General Douglas MacArthur, the hero of the United States' successful Pacific campaign in World War II, they forced the North Koreans to retreat. MacArthur ordered his troops to continue their offen-sive north of the 38th parallel.

MacArthur's troops in North Korea pushed north. As fighting approached the Chinese border, some U.N. com-manders worried about how China would react. MacArthur, however, was convinced that there would be no response from the Chinese. In late October 1950, China responded by sending thousands of Chinese troops into North Korea. Chinese officials were worried that U.N. forces would cross the Yalu River into China. Catching U.N. troops by surprise, the Chinese helped North Korea drive U.N. forces back into South Korea.

The war would rage for nearly three more years. It would claim the lives of more than 1 million soldiers and at least 2 million civilians. Seoul, Inchon, and other cities were reduced to ruins. North Korea and South Korea would sign a ceasefire treaty in June 1953, bringing an end to the fighting. The treaty also reestablished the 38th parallel as the approximate border between North and South Korea. Korea has remained divided ever since.

THE WAR'S IMPACT

China's entry into the Korean War had a significant impact on the U.S. economy and on its domestic and foreign policies. Most Americans assumed that the war would end quickly. Early in the war, MacArthur had confidently asserted that American troops would be home "for Christmas dinner."[1] When the Chi-nese entered the conflict, however, it became clear that it would be a much longer and more expensive war than anticipated.

The war—and the sudden change in its outlook—helped Republicans pick up seats in the Senate and House of

Representatives in the 1950 election. Although Democrats managed to maintain slim majorities in both houses, Republicans regained some power. They began questioning the policies of the Truman administration more vigorously. Republicans were able to oppose the administration and congressional Democrats successfully on a range of issues, including government regulations, spending on social programs, and foreign policy. A number of conservative Republicans began advocating a return to isolationism, the U.S. foreign policy that had been in place since the presidency of George Washington and had endured up until World War II.

Congress had always strongly supported the Marshall Plan. It had passed the budgets for the Marshall Plan with little debate. The Truman administration had succeeded in making the case that the United States could afford to provide aid for European recovery. Business and labor leaders believed that the Marshall Plan helped prevent the collapse of European markets for American goods. By strengthening Western Europe's economy and helping unify Western Europe, the Marshall Plan was also viewed as a sensible alternative to spending huge amounts of money on defense in order to address the communist threat in Europe.

As the Korean War's impact on the U.S. economy became evident, however, congressional support waivered. The large increase in military spending led to domestic shortages of such raw materials as steel, rubber, and gasoline. As more and more resources were diverted to the war effort, prices for goods in the United State rose. The notion that the United States could afford the Marshall Plan became a matter of debate.

The first blow to the Marshall Plan came in December 1950. Although its economic recovery still lagged behind most of the other Marshall Plan nations, the United Kingdom decided to end its participation in the European Recovery Program. The British public had never warmed to the idea of accepting aid from the United States, despite the longtime economic and political ties between the two nations. Government officials felt that it was time for the country to rely on itself. The United Kingdom also was more reluctant than the other Marshall Plan countries to cooperate with the OEEC. In a letter to George Marshall, Ernest Bevin wrote: "I sat in the House of Commons yesterday and heard the chancellor announce the suspension of Marshall aid, and had you been there I should have wanted to go and say to you with a full heart 'thank you.'"[2]

The Korean War also had a major impact in Western Europe. The invasion of South Korea by Soviet-backed North Korean troops heightened fears of communist aggression. Governments in Western Europe began to assess their military preparedness. Most felt extremely vulnerable to the powerful Soviet army and its rearmed Eastern European allies. Since the end of World War II, nearly all of the Western European governments had focused the majority of their funds and energy into rebuilding their countries and providing social services to their citizens. Little money had been allocated to weapons and military training.

Although the United States was bogged down in the war in Korea, building up military defenses in Europe soon became a priority for President Truman. The United States began insisting that the Marshall Plan nations strengthen NATO, which had been founded two years earlier to provide for the common defense of Western Europe. The Americans wanted Western Europe to build a strong barrier to protect itself against the Soviet Union and its Eastern European satellites.

The Truman administration also began pressuring Western Europe to allow West Germany to rearm itself. Officials pointed out that the Soviet Union was supplying weapons and training to the East Germans. Soviet troops were even stationed in East Germany. The United States argued that West Germans should be allowed to rearm to protect themselves from the communist threat. Because West Germany was quickly rebuilding its industrial capacity, it had the potential to be an important part of Western Europe's overall defense strategy.

On April 18, 1951, representatives from Belgium, France, Italy, Luxembourg, and the Netherlands met in Paris. They invited the West German government to attend the meeting. The

THE END OF THE MARSHALL PLAN

On December 30, 1951, the ECA released a statement to the media. It summarized the efforts and successes of the agency in implementing the Marshall Plan:

> The American people tomorrow close the books on the most daring and constructive venture in peace-time international relations the world has ever seen: The Marshall Plan. . . . "When future historians look back upon the achievements of the Marshall Plan," [acting ECA Administrator Richard] Bissell said, "I believe they will see in it the charge that blasted the first substantial cracks in the centuries-old walls of European nationalism—walls that once destroyed will clear the way for the building of a unified, prosperous, and, above all, peaceful continent."
>
> . . . For the first time in history, governments of 18 free nations of Europe banded together to work out common solutions to common economic problems and make the best possible use of American aid. Thanks largely to the efforts of the OEEC, some 75 percent of the restrictions which formerly hampered the free movement of goods between countries of Europe have now been removed, and the volume of intra-European trade is now virtually double what it was in 1947.

six nations signed an agreement known as the Schuman Treaty (or the Treaty of Paris). It created a partnership between the nations that further united the economies of Western Europe. The Schuman Treaty created a single, common market for steel and coal in the six participating countries. Member countries

. . . There are still many dark spots in Europe's economic picture. Darkest of all is the widening dollar gap brought on by the inflationary pressures of the free world's rearmament effort. It is a dollar gap that makes mandatory continued economic aid to Europe through the burdensome period of rearmament. But the free world's leaders are convinced that the economic and moral foundation rebuilt by Europe in the past 4 years with the help of the American people through the Marshall Plan will hold firm.

The vision of a new Europe, economically strong, unified as it had never been before, standing resolutely in the ranks of the free countries of the world, has become a fact.

Tomorrow, that chapter of American history which made this possible—the Marshall Plan—is finished. Heavily criticized by some; labeled "the give-away program" by many, it has had the continuous support of the Congress, industry, labor, and nearly every other segment of American life.

To them, the American people who have supported it, belongs whatever verdict is handed down by the unbiased eyes of future history.*

* *Department of State Bulletin*, Washington, D.C.: U.S. Government Printing Office, Vol. XXVI, No. 655, Publication 4457, January 14, 1952. http://www.archive.org/stream/departmentofstat2652unit/departmentofstat2652unit_djvu.txt.

agreed to give up control of the production of steel and coal within their national borders and handed over these rights to a new agency, the European Coal and Steel Community.

The Schuman Treaty laid the groundwork for future economic programs to reduce import quotas and to boost productivity. It would also provide a foundation for the creation of the European Economic Community (EEC) in 1957 and the European Union (EU) in 1993. Most importantly, the Schuman Treaty welcomed West Germany into the community of Western European nations. The former enemy of the Allies would eventually participate in the common defense of Western Europe. By joining together, these six nations improved their ability to stand up to the Soviets.

Slowly, the Truman administration transformed the Marshall Plan from a program providing economic aid to one providing military aid. The ECA continued to administer the funds for economic aid. The Defense Department was given control of the funds for military aid. The diversion of Marshall Plan funds from economic aid to military aid had an unfortunate side effect: It weakened Western European economies. Prices soared, and the dollar gap in some countries began to widen again. In addition to being upset by the cuts to economic aid, Europeans became increasingly frustrated with the U.S. government. They questioned U.S. involvement in the Korean War, considering it irresponsible. They also worried that the heightened tensions between the United States and the Soviet Union would draw them into a conflict with the Soviets.

Although they preferred economic aid to military aid, Marshall Plan countries accepted the military aid packages offered by the United States. They also increased their own military spending to rebuild their militaries. By increasing military spending during a worsening economy, however, government officials strengthened their political opponents. In 1951, the communist parties in France and Italy made strong comebacks in those countries' elections.

Secretary of State Dean Acheson later noted, "For some time in 1951 it had been dawning on us that we were trying to move our allies and ourselves faster toward the rearmament for defense than economic realities would permit. It made no sense to destroy them in the name of defending them."[3] Near the end of 1951, the Truman administration decided to adjust the ratio between military and economic aid. It transferred $550 million from the military aid budget into the economic aid program.

In mid-1951, Truman asked Congress to pass the Mutual Security Act, authorizing a total of $8.6 billion for foreign aid. The budget would be split between military aid ($6.1 billion) and economic aid ($2.5 billion). Although Congress agreed to the administration's budget for military aid, it authorized only $1.5 billion for economic aid. Congress also created an agency to administer all U.S. foreign aid—both military and economic. The Mutual Security Administration (MSA) would take over the functions of the ECA. After Truman signed the bill on October 15, 1951, the president appointed Averell Harriman as director of the MSA.

When adopted in 1948, the Marshall Plan had been scheduled to expire on June 30, 1952. The Korean War and politics shut it down six months early. The ECA ended its operations on December 31, 1951. In the closing statement of the ECA, its director, Richard Bissell, wrote, "It was the ECA's success in reviving Europe that had made a reduction of its activities possible in the first place."[4] Many ECA employees stayed on to work for the MSA. Through the MSA, the United States continued to send economic aid to Europe for the next several years. The Marshall Plan, however, had come to its end.

The Impact of the Marshall Plan

When George Marshall made his now-historic speech at Harvard University in 1947, chaos and despair gripped postwar Europe. Its cities and farms lay in ruins. Governments were in disarray and lacked resources to help their citizens. Many people were homeless, jobless, and hungry. Congress passed the Marshall Plan legislation to finance an economic-recovery plan. The plan would be drafted by representatives of 16 Western European countries. ERP funds would be used to provide humanitarian aid, finance rebuilding, and increase agricultural and industrial production in Western Europe.

Between April 1948 and December 1951, the ERP supplied about $13 billion in aid—an amount equal to about $100 billion in today's dollars. Marshall Plan aid accounted for about 2 percent of the United States' gross national product during that period. (Gross national product is the total value of all goods and services produced by a country during a certain time period, usually a year.) In comparison, the United States now spends about 0.4 percent of its gross national product on foreign aid. The 16 Marshall Plan countries spent about $9 billion of their own money to finance relief and recovery projects.

THE ECONOMIC EFFECT

Most Marshall Plan funds were distributed in four major aid categories. About $5.2 billion was spent to buy food and other agricultural goods, such as cotton. About $5.5 billion was spent to buy raw materials and other industrial goods. More than $800 million was used to pay shipping companies to transport the goods to Europe. The United States contributed nearly $500 million to help Europeans set up and operate the European Payments Union. The EPU helped improve trade among the Marshall Plan countries by avoiding the currency problems caused by trade imbalances. About two-thirds of all ERP aid went to four countries: the United Kingdom (25 percent), France (20 percent), Italy (10 percent), and West Germany (10 percent).

When the Marshall Plan ended on the last day of 1951, the economic transformation in Marshall Plan countries was striking. Increases in the production of basic goods demonstrated the strength of the recovery:

- ✧ Overall industrial production increased 64 percent (41 percent above prewar levels).
- ✧ Electrical production increased 100 percent.
- ✧ Steel production increased nearly 100 percent.
- ✧ Coal production increased 27 percent (slightly below prewar levels).
- ✧ Aluminum production increased 69 percent.
- ✧ Copper production increased 31 percent.
- ✧ Cement production increased 90 percent.
- ✧ Motor vehicle production increased 37 percent.
- ✧ Cotton production increased 65 percent.

In total, the collective gross national products of the Marshall Plan countries rose by nearly 25 percent between 1947 and 1951. Food production had increased 27 percent over the 1947 level (and 9 percent above prewar levels). Western Europe still did not produce enough food to feed itself. Populations in these nations were also growing faster than the increases in food productions. Since 1947, the total population in Marshall Plan countries grew from 250 million to 275 million.

By the end of 1951, Marshall Plan countries had used nearly $500 million of ERP aid funds to finance 132 large industrial projects. The nations completed or made substantial progress on 27 major power plant projects, 32 projects for updating and expanding iron and steel plants, and 62 other major industrial projects. (The ECA considered any project costing more than $1 million a major project.) The countries also built 11 major petroleum refining works, resulting in a 400 percent increase in fuel production.

Counterpart funds helped pay for many major infrastructure and transportation projects, particularly in France, Italy, and West Germany. With ECA approval, these funds were used to improve electric, gas, and other public utility facilities. Marshall Plan countries also used about $500 million in counterpart funds to rebuild and modernize the continent's war-damaged railway system. Other counterpart funds were used to build or improve airports and to reconstruct merchant fleets, port and shipping facilities, and inland waterways. Some countries, particularly the United Kingdom and Norway, used counterpart funds to pay off government debts.

At the time, American officials on both sides of the Atlantic trumpeted that the Marshall Plan had saved Europe from economic ruin. Some Europeans, however, thought that its impact was being overstated. Critics of the Marshall Plan pointed out that European recovery was already in progress when ERP aid began flowing in mid-1948. Others believed that the Marshall Plan was less about economic aid than it

A young girl holds balloons that carry a message of peace to countries in Eastern Europe at the spring fair in Vienna, Austria, in 1951. More than 50,000 balloons were released with the message *Marshall Plan 1951 Friede, Freiheit, Wohlstand* ("Peace, Freedom, Welfare"). A postcard attached to each expressed the hope that "someday goods and products will flow freely across the countries of a united and prosperous Europe."

was about U.S. political and military strategies in the emerging Cold War.

While most Europeans were grateful for Marshall Plan aid, others were less enthusiastic about its consequences. European companies complained that U.S. companies were taking over their markets. A British politician agreed, grousing that the Marshall Plan was merely a program that allowed "the Yankee businessman's invasions of Europe!"[1] Italian labor leaders complained that workers had benefited little from the Marshall Plan. In his travels around Western Europe, American journalist Theodore White observed, "The rich and well-to-do rolled about once more in automobiles. . . . But the workers had barely held their own; they lived in stinking, festering slums; dressed in shabby second-hand clothes."[2]

The Marshall Plan was not the sole reason that Western Europe's economy made such a remarkable recovery. Many other factors also played major roles in the rebuilding effort. An outstanding harvest during the 1948 growing season boosted agricultural production in Marshall Plan countries. To contribute to their nations' recoveries, Western European workers did not ask for higher wages or go on strike, despite facing increasing prices for everyday items. Many new companies were started without the help of ERP aid. The launch of a new currency in West Germany helped jumpstart its economy. Rearmament and military programs also helped fuel Western Europe's economic expansion.

The most crucial economic effect of the Marshall Plan was to help Europe get though a period of extreme economic instability. During its first 18 months, the ERP provided aid to Europe that helped reduce critical shortages of such key goods as food, fuel, machinery, and steel. The aid not only helped reduce the dollar gap, it also enabled Marshall Plan countries to increase their imports and use their own money for reconstruction projects. Technical assistance provided by the Marshall Plan helped European industries and businesses improve worker productivity. Historian Charles Maier summed up the economic impact of the Marshall Plan in Europe: "U.S. aid served . . . like the lubricant in an engine—not the fuel—allowing a machine to run that would otherwise buckle and bind."[3] ERP aid enabled Marshall Plan countries to revive their economies without cutting spending on social programs, which helped people survive the hard times. It also allowed them to avoid ordering wage cuts, which would help lower inflation.

POLITICAL CONSEQUENCES

The political consequences of the Marshall Plan were more enduring than its economic successes. Like most U.S. foreign aid programs, the ERP was created to advance America's foreign policy and national security goals. The Truman administration designed the Marshall Plan to help support weakening democracies in Europe. It achieved that goal. ERP aid helped democratic governments hold on to power in Marshall Plan countries during the difficult period from 1947 to 1949. Government leaders in these countries were able to point out the economic progress that the Marshall Plan promised.

Communist coups, such as the ones that had occurred in Czechoslovakia and Hungary, were unlikely to occur in Western Europe. Communist parties competed with democratic parties in many Marshall Plan countries, particularly in France, Italy, and Greece. Moderate parties in those three countries were able to defeat Communist Party candidates in elections. In its closing statement, the ECA noted that

> the expansion of communism in Western Europe has been
> abruptly halted and the tide sharply turned back in the years
> of the Marshall Plan. In country after country, free elections
> have seen the Communist Party overwhelmed almost to the
> point of extinction. In France and Italy, while Communist-
> dominated unions still hold the biggest bloc of workers,
> their membership losses have been staggering. In France, it

In August 1961, West Berliners (*right*) watch their East German counterparts erect a wall in West Berlin to prevent people from leaving East Germany. Built with barbed wire and concrete, the Berlin Wall, as it would come to be known, ultimately stretched for about 30 miles. A symbol of the Cold War that divided East and West, it stood for 28 years. The wall was torn down after communism collapsed in Eastern Europe in 1989.

is estimated that the powerful CGT [labor union] has lost from half a million to three million members. In Italy, the Communist-dominated CGIL [labor union] has lost about 2.5 million members.[4]

In order to receive Marshall Plan aid, Western European nations had to work together to create a recovery plan. The diplomatic successes of the 1947 Paris Conference motivated Western European nations to work together to solve common problems. They began to consider each other as partners. Through the OEEC and the European Coal and Steel Community, Western Europe achieved its first successes at economic cooperation. Marshall Plan countries eased trade restrictions by agreeing to reduce or eliminate import tariffs. They also created the EPU, which helped make it easier for the Marshall Plan countries to avoid trade imbalances. All of these agreements and new organizations formed the foundation for greater economic integration in the decades to come.

The Marshall Plan was also a key factor in easing West Germany back into the family of Western European nations. Political pressure and economic incentives from the United States and other Marshall Plan countries coaxed France into giving up its determination to make Germany pay war reparations. French officials realized that ERP aid was more useful to them than any reparations that they could eventually squeeze out of war-torn Germany. They even proposed unifying their coal and steel production with Germany's, which led to the creation of the European Coal and Steel Community.

The Marshall Plan exposed the growing tensions between the United States and the Soviet Union. The ERP abruptly divided Europe into Western and Eastern blocs, hardening the divisions between the democratic Western European nations and communist Eastern European nations. Nowhere was the divide more apparent than in Germany. The country was split, with the former U.S., British, and French occupation zones making up West Germany and the former Soviet occupation zone making up East Germany. (Unlike Germany, Austria successfully emerged undivided from its occupation by the United States, the United Kingdom, France, and the Soviet Union as an independent democracy.) Although surrounded by East Germany, West Berlin would remain part of West Germany. It

A NEW GERMANY

After the military defeat of Germany in 1945, the Allies divided Germany—and its capital, Berlin—into four occupation zones. By 1948, the growing rift between the Soviet Union and its three former allies had made the Soviets uncooperative in efforts to reunite all four zones into a new German state. It had become clear to all that Germany, like Korea, would remain divided. The United States, the United Kingdom, and France decided that their three occupation zones should be united into a new nation.

In late 1948 and early 1949, German representatives from the American, English, and French zones met in Bonn, Germany, where they drafted and approved a constitution, called the *Grundgesetz* ("Basic Law"). It would govern a new democratic nation called the Federal Republic of Germany, or West Germany. On May 23, 1949, the Federal Republic of Germany was born. In nationwide elections, the Christian Democrat party received the majority of votes. Konrad Adenauer became the nation's first chancellor, or leader. Following the elections, the ERP provided about $1.3 billion in aid to the new country. The Marshall Plan, however, had less impact in West Germany than in most other Marshall Plan nations since it received a lower amount of would endure as one of the most visible symbols of the Cold War for nearly three decades.

Committing money to the Marshall Plan was also the first step in America's shift away from its traditional foreign policy of isolationism. As a result, the United States developed a much closer relationship with Western Europe than it previously

aid because it was in the program for a shorter amount of time. Also, its economy was so large that ERP funds had less of an effect on West Germany's overall economy.

Before and during World War II, Germany had been an industrial powerhouse. In 1949, West Germany quickly began to reestablish its industrial might. Despite heavy bombing during the war, many West German industrial facilities remained intact or had suffered only moder- ate damage. By 1952, West Germany achieved the second largest level of industrial production in Western Europe. Despite losing the output of Germany's richest farmlands, located in what was then East Germany, West Germany significantly increased its food production. Its complete recovery, however, would take more time. The young nation still had to import food to feed its people and raw materials to supply its factories.

In an August 1949 interview published in *Life*, a U.S. magazine, Adenauer pledged that "in the years to come an economically and politically healthy [West] Germany, indebted for the aid from the West, may eventually repay these commitments by contributing her share to the benefit of the Atlantic world to which we all belong."*

* Quoted in Greg Behrman, *The Most Noble Adventure*, New York: Free Press, 2007, p. 267.

had. The Marshall Plan transformed from an economic-aid program into a program to provide military aid and speed up rearmament in Europe. The rearmament led to the formation of NATO. The Marshall Plan soon turned the Marshall Plan countries into partners. The increased presence of the United States in Europe demonstrated its new role as a world power. The United States began to expand its relationships with more nations, using its enormous influence to shape economies, politics, and military conflicts around the world.

PSYCHOLOGICAL IMPACT

The Marshall Plan's greatest impact may have been to provide optimism to Europeans when all seemed to be lost. The freighters that began to arrive in European ports in the spring of 1948 brought more than just food, tractors, machinery, and raw materials. They reenergized the governments and people of Western Europe. The four-year assistance program offered by the Marshall Plan created optimism where there had been only doubt. It motivated European leaders to create a recovery plan for their economy. It encouraged entrepreneurs to create businesses.

For the homeless, the unemployed, the hungry, and the disheartened, the Marshall Plan provided the one thing that they needed the most—hope for the future. In 1949, the United Kingdom's prime minister, Clement Attlee, wrote to President Truman, declaring that ERP aid "gave us hope and help when we most needed it. During the last year the whole economic scene in Western Europe has been transformed to a degree which must astonish all of us when we recall the uncertainties and perils of the immediately preceding year."[5]

The Legacy of the Marshall Plan

ormer Prime Minister Winston Churchill of Great Britain called the success of the Marshall Plan "a turning point in the history of the world."[1] This was not just empty rhetoric. The Marshall Plan had consequences on European society—and the rest of the planet—that continue to be felt to this day. For Europe, it meant a new level of cooperation and mutual trust that is unrivaled in its history. For the world, it demonstrated that often difficult and contentious international problems could be dealt with diplomatically, in an effectively short period, without resulting in warfare or chaos.

EUROPEAN UNIFICATION

In designing the Marshall Plan, the Truman administration had two central economic goals. The first was to provide temporary aid to help Europe's teetering postwar economy recover.

The economic recovery improved the daily lives of Europeans and helped produce political stability.

The administration's second economic goal was to promote economic cooperation among Western European countries, which in turn would foster better relations between nations. Although Marshall Plan countries were reluctant to give up any control over their own economies, they eventually agreed with ECA officials that Western Europe needed to create a larger, unified market in order to achieve long-term economic growth. Through the creation of the OEEC, the European Coal and Steel Community, and the European Payments Union, the Marshall Plan countries began integrating their economies in key economic sectors. These regional organizations were the forerunners of stronger economic—and political—unification efforts in Western Europe.

In 1957, the six countries that made up the ECSC—Belgium, France, Italy, Luxembourg, the Netherlands, and West Germany—signed the Treaty of Rome. The treaty created the European Economic Community, popularly known as the Common Market. The EEC's mission was to allow people, goods, and services to move freely across the borders of the six nations by eliminating trade barriers. Ten years later, the EEC and the ECSC merged. More Western European nations joined the EEC. Denmark, Ireland, and the United Kingdom became members in 1972, increasing EEC membership to nine. New members Greece (1979), Portugal (1985), and Spain (1985) expanded EEC membership to 12 countries.

In 1992, the 12 EEC countries signed the 1992 Treaty of Maastricht, transforming the EEC into a new organization, the European Union. The agreement provided the foundation for more extensive cooperation on organizational matters, legal issues, foreign affairs, and defense policies. It also expanded economic unification, including the creation of a currency—the euro. Another European treaty, the Treaty of Rome, declared that the member nations were

50 YEARS LATER — BLUEPRINTS FOR THE RECOVERY OF EUROPE

The Marshall Plan

The U.S. plan which funded post-war Europe from April 3, 1948 to June 30, 1952 helped bolster the overseas economy. A look:

Aid in millions of dollars
% increase per capita GDP (1938-65)

European boundaries in 1947 (Iceland GDP excluded)

*Belgium-Luxembourg
**Belgium

State of post-war Europe

Food
- The winter of 1946-47 was one of the harshest; harvests poor
- Fertilizer, machinery shortages
- People in Southern and Eastern Europe brought to minimal subsistence levels

Finances
- Governments had financed the war and are unable to pay for imports
- Domestic inflation soars from limited supplies
- By 1947 grants and loans begin to dry up

Coal
- Europe derived 80 percent of its energy from coal
- Western coal zones at less than a third of prewar output by the end 1948
- Steel production curtailed; machinery production drops off

On June 5, 1947 Secretary of State George C. Marshall outlined a recovery plan to revitalize war-torn Western Europe. President Harry Truman asked Congress for $17 billion over four years. Congress granted $13.3 billion. The plan:

Objectives
- Increasing production
- Expanding European trade
- Facilitating European economic cooperation and integration
- Controlling inflation

Approach
- 16 countries formed the Committee of European Economic Cooperation; countries' needs were evaluated and reported. The Soviets pressured eastern countries to boycott.
- President of Studebaker Paul Hoffman headed the U.S. Economic Cooperation Administration

Soviet reaction
- Disturbed by the success of the Marshall plan, the Soviets blockaded the corridor between West Germany and Berlin in June 1948. Food and supplies to 2-1/2 million people were cut off
- Supplies were airlifted; the blockade ended May 12, 1949

Recovery increases in 1950
- Agricultural output: 11 percent
- Industrial production: 40 percent
- Intra-European trade: 24 percent

George C. Marshall
(1880-1959)
- U.S. Army chief of staff
- Secretary of state
- Originator of the European Recovery plan
- Secretary of defense
- Nobel Peace Prize

Per capita GDP (In dollars)

$13,495
$13,316
$12,000
Europe (Avg.)
United States
9,000
6,000
1938   1947 1951   1965

SOURCES: George C. Marshall Foundation, Organization of Economic Cooperation and Development

'Our deepest concern is reviving the economy and viability of Western Europe.'   —President Harry Truman

This graphic, created to mark the fiftieth anniversary of the Marshall Plan in 1997, shows the plan's objectives and goals, as well as the levels of aid given to each country.

determined to lay the foundations of an ever closer union among the peoples of Europe, resolved to ensure the economic and social progress of their countries by common action to

eliminate the barriers which divide Europe, affirming as the
essential objective of their efforts the constant improvements
of the living and working conditions of their peoples.[2]

The EU was based on what it called the Four Freedoms: the free
movement of people, goods, services, and capital.

In 1994, the EU welcomed three new members: Austria,
Finland, and Sweden. It eventually expanded its reach beyond
Western Europe. In 2003, Cyprus, the Czech Republic, Estonia,
Hungary, Latvia, Lithuania, Poland, Slovakia, and Slovenia
joined the EU. Two years later, Bulgaria and Romania expanded
the EU's membership to 27 nations. Negotiations are in progress to admit Turkey as a member nation.

The EU's transformation from a six-nation cooperative
agreement focused on coal and steel to a powerful 27-nation
organization is a remarkable achievement. With a population
of about 500 million, the union accounts for nearly one-third
of the world's economic production. The EU's unification of
Western and Eastern European countries would have been
unthinkable during the Cold War. It would have surprised even
the most optimistic Marshall Plan policymakers in the Truman
administration. On the fiftieth anniversary of the Marshall Plan
in 1997, former German Chancellor Helmut Schmidt observed
that the "European Union is one of its . . . greatest achievements:
it would never have happened without the Marshall Plan."[3]

EUROPEAN SECURITY

Financial recovery in Western European countries helped create
political stability. It also led to greater cooperation in creating a
common military defense. With the United States–Soviet Union
relationship crumbling, the Truman administration wanted
the Marshall Plan countries to start contributing to their own
defense and as a result began shifting Marshall Plan aid funds
to European rearmament programs. Because of its own national
security interests, the United States made a larger commitment

to Western Europe. A transatlantic defense partnership grew, culminating in the creation of NATO in April 1949. NATO's mission was to provide for the mutual defense of its members. Its original 12 members were Belgium, Canada, Denmark, France, Iceland, Italy, Luxembourg, the Netherlands, Norway, Portugal, the United Kingdom, and the United States. Headquartered in Brussels, Belgium, NATO has since expanded to 28 members.

U.S. FOREIGN AID

The foreign policy goals of the Marshall Plan had compelled the Truman administration to assume a larger role in Europe. The successes of the European aid program encouraged the United States to move beyond its prewar isolationism, and it increased its interactions with other nations. As the Cold War heated up, the United States began to flex its muscles as a world superpower. Economic aid programs became a vital part of U.S. foreign policy.

In his January 1949 inaugural address, President Truman announced that four major objectives would guide U.S. foreign policy: supporting the mission of the United Nations, continuing the European recovery program (the Marshall Plan), helping nations resist threats to their sovereignty (through NATO and other alliances), and launching a new foreign-aid program. With the fourth objective, Truman was proposing a new direction for U.S. foreign policy. He wanted the United States to "embark on a bold new program for making the benefits of our scientific advances and industrial progress available for the improvement and growth of underdeveloped areas."[4]

Truman believed that the lack of aid programs outside of Western Europe weakened U.S. foreign policy in those regions. To promote economic growth in developing countries around the world, the administration launched the Point Four program, named after the fourth point in Truman's inaugural address, in 1949. The program was conceived as a joint public-private venture, with funding coming from the U.S. government and private businesses. U.S. policymakers viewed developing countries as a good source of raw materials to supply U.S. industry and as an untapped market for U.S. exports. State Department officials saw the promotion of economic growth as a way to encourage democracies in developing countries and prevent the spread of communism worldwide. From the beginning, the Point Four program suffered from lack of funding. It received only $20 million from Congress. Private enterprise also showed little enthusiasm for the program.

To overcome the shortcomings of the Point Four program, the administration next proposed that a new U.N. agency be created to provide technical assistance to developing countries. In 1950, the Expanded Program of Technical Assistance (EPTA) began its operations. Supervised by the U.N.'s Economic and Social Council, the agency sent industrial and agricultural experts to developing countries to teach skills, such as ways to improve productivity. The United States provided more than half of EPTA's initial funding. EPTA eventually grew into the United Nations Development Program, which continues to provide assistance to developing countries.

In the Foreign Assistance Act of 1961, passed during the presidency of John F. Kennedy, Congress provided funding for a new foreign-aid agency in the executive branch. The United States Agency for International Development (USAID) was given the mission to support long-term economic growth worldwide and to advance U.S. foreign policy goals. Embracing the ideals of the Marshall Plan, USAID provides assistance to developing nations that are making efforts to expand their economies and pursuing democratic reforms. It also provides aid to countries recovering from natural disasters. USAID provides aid in five regions of the world: sub-Saharan Africa, Asia, Europe and Eurasia, Latin American and the Caribbean, and the Middle East.

USAID has experienced mixed results. Although it has helped many countries strengthen their economies and has boosted the influence of the United States worldwide, USAID has been never been able to match the success and influence of the Marshall Plan. Progress in development has been slow in all five regions. Economic inefficiencies and government corruption in developing nations have curbed the impact of USAID assistance. Some countries have become dependent on American aid. Instead of using the USAID assistance as a resource to promote economic growth, these countries have come to view USAID funds as part of their economies.

THE GERMAN MARSHALL FUND

In 1972, Chancellor Willy Brandt of West Germany gave a speech at Harvard University. In his address, he announced a plan to honor the Marshall Plan and its assistance to postwar Europe. "The memory of the past," Brandt said, "has become the mission of the future."[5] On behalf of its people, the West German government provided funds to create the German Marshall Fund (GMF). Its mission would be to promote cooperation and greater understanding between Europe and the United States.

The GMF sponsors conferences on transatlantic issues and provides grants to people and organizations who conduct research on transatlantic issues. It also organizes meetings to bring government and business leaders together to discuss ways to take action to solve common problems, such as global warming. After the Berlin Wall fell in 1989, GMF began working to strengthen emerging democracies in Central and Eastern Europe.

The GMF, headquartered in Washington, D.C., has seven offices in Europe: Ankara, Turkey; Belgrade, Serbia; Berlin; Bratislava, Slovakia; Brussels; Turin, Italy; Bucharest, Romania; and Paris. The German government provided addition funds in 1986 and 2001 to ensure that the GMF could continue its mission. It also receives grants from the EU, the USAID, and private foundations.

LOOKING BACK AND LOOKING AHEAD

In 2007, people around the world celebrated the sixtieth anniversary of George Marshall's Harvard speech. The Organization

A giant Euro tree towers above a crowd at a euro party in Maastricht, Netherlands, on January 1, 2002, the first year the new currency would be issued. Greater economic coordination and a unifying legal tender in European nations were among the main goals of the Marshall Plan. Today, the euro is the sole currency in 17 nations in the Eurozone.

for Economic Cooperation and Development (OECD), the agency that took over for the OEEC in 1961, joined with the U.S. government to sponsor a conference in Paris to commemorate the impact of the Marshall Plan. The conference, titled "Lessons Learned Applicable to the 21st Century," was held at the Hôtel de Talleyrand, the same building that housed Averell Harriman's OSR offices during the years of the Marshall Plan. There, scholars, government officials, business leaders, and other speakers discussed how the lessons of the Marshall Plan could be applied to economic and political challenges in the twenty-first century.

In the introductory address at the conference, Constance A. Morella, the U.S. ambassador to the OECD, stated:

> Among the secrets for the success of the Marshall Plan . . . was the spirit of cooperation evidenced in its execution. The program was truly a joint European–American venture, one in which American resources were complemented with local resources and all the participants worked cooperatively toward the common goals of freedom and prosperity.[6]

She continued, "Thanks to the Marshall Plan, not only did the countries of Europe become closer together, but Europe and the United States also became inextricably linked. Today, this transatlantic partnership still exists and faces new global challenges that require us to work together as never before."[7]

In its 1951 closing statement, the ECA asserted, "Never in human history has so much been spent by so few with such great results."[8] The successes of the Marshall Plan had a profound effect on both sides of the Atlantic. In Europe, it encouraged increased cooperation on economic matters, which led to the creation of the European Union. In the United States, it convinced policymakers that economic aid could be used to achieve foreign policy goals. It helped bring countries on both sides of the Atlantic together to form a mutual defense agreement, leading to the creation of NATO.

During its 31-month existence, the Marshall Plan brought together politicians, policymakers, business leaders, and workers throughout Western Europe and the United States. It asked them to make many sacrifices, to remain optimistic during the darkest times, and to carry on when it would have been easy to give up. Together, they persevered and provided the necessary answers to the challenging questions posed by George Marshall on that June afternoon in Cambridge, Massachusetts: "What is needed? What can best be done? What must be done?"[9]

1947   June 5 George Marshall calls for a European recovery
        plan.

        July 12 Conference for European Nations meets in Paris.

        September 23 16 Marshall Plan countries submit a draft
        recovery plan to the United States.

1948   February A Soviet-backed communist coup seizes power
        in Czechoslovakia.

        April 2 Congress passes the Foreign Assistance Act,
        authorizing the European Recovery Program also known

TIMELINE

1947
June 5 George Marshall
calls for a European
recovery plan.

1948
February A Soviet-backed communist
coup seizes power in Czechoslovakia.

1947

1948

July 12 Conference for
European Nations meets
in Paris.
September 23 16 Marshall
Plan countries submit a
draft recovery plan to the
United States.

April 2 Congress passes the Foreign
Assistance Act, authorizing the
Marshall Plan. President Harry
Truman signs it into law the next day.
April Paul Hoffman is appointed
administrator of the ECA. Averell
Harriman is appointed special
representative of the ECA in Europe.

as the Marshall Plan. President Harry Truman signs it into law the next day.

April Paul Hoffman is appointed administrator of the Economic Cooperative Administration. Averell Harriman is appointed special representative of the ECA in Europe.

1949   June 30 West Germany officially enters the Marshall Plan.

1950   June 15 The Korean War begins.

1951   December 31 The ERP ends six months early.

1953   December 10 George Marshall is awarded the Nobel Peace Prize.

1949
June 30 West Germany officially enters the Marshall Plan.

1957
March 25 The European Economic Community is established.

1949

1993

1951
December 31 The ERP ends six months early.

1993
November 1 The European Union is established.

1953
December 10 George Marshall is awarded the Nobel Peace Prize.

1957   March 25 The European Economic Community is established.

1972   July 5 Chancellor Willy Brandt of West Germany announces the creation of the German Marshall Fund.

1993   November 1 The European Union is established.

2007   June The sixtieth anniversary of the Marshall Plan is celebrated.

NOTES

CHAPTER 1

1. Forrest C. Pogue, *George C. Marshall: Organizer of Victory* (New York: Viking, 1963), p. ix.

2. Anne O'Hare McCormick, "Abroad; The Shrouded Future of the Battlefield Once Europe," *New York Times*, March 14, 1945, p. 18.

3. Winston Churchill, Speech in Zurich, Switzerland, on September 19, 1946. http://www.churchill-society-london.org.uk/astonish.html.

4. John T. Bethell, "The Ultimate Commencement Address: The Making of George C. Marshall's 'Routine' Speech," *Harvard Magazine*, May 1997. http://harvardmagazine.com/1997/05/marshall.html.

5. George Marshall, "The Marshall Plan Speech." http://www.oecd.org/document/10/0,3746,en_2649_201185_1876938_1_1_1_1,00.html.

6. Ibid.

7. Ibid.

8. Ibid.

9. Ibid.

10. Ibid.

11. Ibid.

CHAPTER 2

1. Alan Bullock, *Ernest Bevin: Foreign Secretary, 1945–51* (New York: Norton, 1983), pp. 404–405.

2. Associated Press, "Marshall's Plan Under Pravda Fire," *New York Times*, June 17, 1947, p. 5.

3. Arthur Vandenberg, *The Private Papers of Senator Vandenberg* (Westport, Conn.: Greenwood Press, 1974), p. 381.

4. Wilfried Loth, *The Division of the World, 1941–1955* (New York: Routledge, 1988), p. 159.

5. Harold Callender, "16 Nation Aid Plan Signed as Leaders Warn of a Collapse," *New York Times*, September 23, 1947, p. 1.

CHAPTER 3

1. Associated Press, "Communist Leader Pledges Drive to Ruin Marshall Plan," *New York Times*, October 23, 1947, p. 1.

2. Ibid.

3. Ibid.

4. Robert A. Pollard, *Economic Security and the Origins of the Cold War, 1945–1950* (New York: Columbia University Press, 1985), p. 147.

5. Reprinted in "Text of Taft Speech Here Listing Objections to Scale of Marshall Plan for Aid To Europe," *New York Times*, November 11, 1947, pp. 20–21.

6. Quoted in John Gimbel, *The Origins of the Marshall Plan* (Palo Alto, Calif.: Stanford University Press, 1976), p. 272.

7. Quoted in Lloyd C. Gardner, *Architects of Illusion* (Chicago: Quadrangle Books, 1970), p. 136.

8. Marshall Testimony of January 8, 1948, United States Foreign Policy for a Post-War Recovery Program Hearings Before the

Committee on Foreign Affairs, United States Senate, Eightieth Congress, First and Second Sessions, (Washington, D.C.: Government Printing Office).

9. Harold B. Hinton, "Aid Bill Is Signed by Truman As Reply to Foes of Liberty," *New York Times*, April 4, 1948.

10. George C. Marshall, Forrest C. Pogue, and Larry I. Bland, *George C. Marshall: Interviews and Reminiscences for Forrest C. Pogue* (Lexington, Va.: G.C. Marshall Foundation, 1991), p. 556.

CHAPTER 4

1. Greg Behrman, *The Most Noble Adventure* (New York: Free Press, 2007), p. 184.

2. Ibid., p. 175.

3. Ibid., p. 182.

4. Harry Bayard Price, *The Marshall Plan and Its Meaning* (Ithaca, N.Y.: Cornell University Press, 1955), p. 85.

5. John Man, *Berlin Blockade* (New York: Ballantine, 1973), p. 43.

6. G. John Ikenberry, *After Victory: Institutions, Strategic Restraint, and the Building of Order After Major Wars* (Princeton, N.J.: Princeton University Press, 2000), p. 201.

7. Greg Behrman, *The Most Noble Adventure: The Marshall Plan and the Time When America Helped Save Europe* (New York: Free Press, 2007), pp. 215–216.

CHAPTER 5

1. Barry Machado, *In Search of a Usable Past: The Marshall Plan and Postwar Reconstruction Today* (Lexington, Va.: George C. Marshall Foundation, 2007), p. 59.

2. Greg Behrman, *The Most Noble Adventure* (New York: Free Press, 2007), p. 251.

3. Eliot Sorel and Pier Carlo Padoan, eds., *The Marshall Plan: Lessons Learned For the 21st Century* (Paris: OECD, 2008), p. 34.

4. Ibid.

5. Michael Hogan, *The Marshall Plan: America, Britain, and the Reconstruction of Western Europe* (New York: Cambridge University Press, 1989), p. 177.

6. Richard M. Bissell, *Reflections of a Cold Warrior* (New Haven, Conn.: Yale University Press, 1996), p. 57.

CHAPTER 6

1. David Halberstam, *The Coldest Winter: America and the Korean War* (New York: Hyperion, 2007), p. 338.

2. Greg Behrman, *The Most Noble Adventure* (New York: Free Press, 2007), p. 309.

3. Dean Acheson, *Present at the Creation: My Years in the State Department* (New York: Norton, 1969), pp. 559–560.

4. Richard M. Bissell, *Reflections of a Cold Warrior* (New Haven, Conn.: Yale University Press, 1996), p. 71.

CHAPTER 7

1. Charles L. Mee Jr., *The Marshall Plan: The Launching of Pax Americana* (New York: Simon & Schuster, 1984), p. 258.

2. Theodore H. White, *Fire in the Ashes* (New York: Sloane, 1968), p.69.

3. Charles Maier, *In Search of Stability: Explorations in Historical Political Economy* (New York: Cambridge University Press, 1988), pp. 341–343.

4. Economic Cooperation Administration news release, December 30, 1951, "Achievements of the Marshall Plan," *Department of State Bulletin* 26 (January 14, 1952), p. 43.

5. Greg Behrman, *The Most Noble Adventure* (New York: Free Press, 2007), p. 252.

CHAPTER 8

1. Martin Gilbert, *Churchill and America* (New York: Simon & Schuster, 2008), p. 389.

2. Preamble, Treaty of Rome. http://www.hri.org/MFA/foreign/treaties/Rome57/BH343.txt.

3. Arthur M. Schlesinger Jr., *A Life in the Twentieth Century* (New York: Houghton Mifflin, 2000), p. 476.

4. Matthew C. Price, *The Advancement of Liberty* (Westport, Conn.: Greenwood, 2008), p. 110.

5. Stanley Hoffman and Charles S. Maier, *The Marshall Plan: A Retrospective* (Boulder, Col.: Westview, 1984), p. 111.

6. Constance A. Morella, "Marshall Plan 60th Anniversary Symposium: Introductory Remarks," in Eliot Sorel and Pier Carlo Padoan, eds., *The Marshall Plan: Lessons Learned for the 21st Century* (Paris: OECD, 2008), p. 6.

7. Ibid.

8. Economic Cooperation Administration news release, December 30, 1951, "Achievements of the Marshall Plan," *Department of State Bulletin* 26 (January 14, 1952), p. 43.

9. George Marshall, "The Marshall Plan Speech." http://www.oecd.org/document/10/0,3746,en_2649_201185_1876938_1_1_1_1,00.html.

BIBLIOGRAPHY

Acheson, Dean. *Present at the Creation: My Years in the State Department.* New York: Norton, 1969.

Associated Press. "Marshall's Plan Under Pravda Fire," *New York Times*, June 17, 1947.

———. "Communist Leader Pledges Drive to Ruin Marshall Plan," *New York Times*, October 23, 1947.

Behrman, Greg. *The Most Noble Adventure: The Marshall Plan and the Time When America Helped Save Europe.* New York: Free Press, 2007.

Bissell, Richard M. *Reflections of a Cold Warrior.* New Haven, Conn.: Yale University Press, 1996.

Bullock, Alan. *Ernest Bevin: Foreign Secretary, 1945–51.* New York: Norton, 1983.

Bethell, John T. "The Ultimate Commencement Address: The Making of George C. Marshall's 'Routine' Speech." *Harvard Magazine*, May 1997. Available online. URL: http://harvardmagazine.com/1997/05/marshall.html.

Callender, Harold. "16 Nation Aid Plan Signed as Leaders Warn of a Collapse." *New York Times*, September 23, 1947.

Churchill, Winston. Speech in Zurich on September 19, 1946. Available online. URL: http://www.churchill-society-london.org.uk/astonish.html.

Economic Cooperation Administration. "Achievements of the Marshall Plan," 26 *Department of State Bulletin* 43. January 14, 1952.

Gardner, Lloyd C. *Architects of Illusion.* Chicago: Quadrangle Books, 1970.

Gilbert, Martin. *Churchill and America.* New York: Simon & Schuster, 2005.

Gimbel, John. *The Origins of the Marshall Plan*. Palo Alto, Calif.: Stanford University Press, 1976.

Halberstam, David. *The Coldest Winter: America and the Korean War*. New York: Hyperion, 2007.

Hoffman, Stanley, and Charles S. Maier. *The Marshall Plan: A Retrospective*. Boulder, Col.: Westview, 1984.

Hogan, Michael. *The Marshall Plan: America, Britain, and the Reconstruction of Western Europe, 1947–1952*. New York: Cambridge University Press, 1987.

Hinton, Harold. "Aid Bill Is Signed by Truman As Reply to Foes of Liberty." *New York Times*, April 4, 1948.

Ikenberry, G. John. *After Victory: Institutions, Strategic Restraint, and the Building of Order After Major Wars*. Princeton, N.J.: Princeton University Press, 2000.

Judt, Tony. *Postwar: A History of Europe Since 1945*. New York: Penguin, 2005.

Loth, Wilfried Loth. *The Division of the World, 1941–1955*. New York: Routledge, 1988.

Machado, Barry. *In Search of a Usable Past: The Marshall Plan and Postwar Reconstruction Today*. Lexington, Va.: George C. Marshall Foundation, 2007.

McCormick, Anne O'Hare. "Abroad; The Shrouded Future of the Battlefield Once Europe." *New York Times*, March 14, 1945.

Maier, Charles. *In Search of Stability: Explorations in Historical Political Economy*. New York: Cambridge University Press, 1988.

Man, John. *Berlin Blockade*. New York, Ballantine, 1973.

Marshall, George. "The Marshall Plan Speech." Available online. URL: http://www.oecd.org/document/10/0,3746,en_2649_201185_1876938_1_1_1_1,00.html.

————. Testimony of January 8, 1948, United States Foreign Policy for a Post-War Recovery Program Hearings Before the Committee on Foreign Affairs, United States Senate, Eightieth Congress, First and Second Sessions. Washington, D.C.: Government Printing Office, 1948.

Marshall, George C., Forrest C. Pogue, and Larry I. Bland. *George C. Marshall: Interviews and Reminiscences for Forrest C. Pogue.* Lexington, Va.: G.C. Marshall Foundation, 1991.

Mee, Charles L. Jr. *The Marshall Plan: The Launching of the Pax Americana.* New York: Simon & Schuster, 1984.

Mills, Nicolas. *Winning the Peace: The Marshall Plan and America's Coming of Age as a Superpower.* Hoboken, N.J.: Wiley, 2008.

Pogue, Forrest C. *George C. Marshall: Organizer of Victory.* New York: Viking, 1963.

Pollard, Robert A. *Economic Security and the Origins of the Cold War, 1945–1950.* New York: Columbia University Press, 1985.

Price, Harry Bayard. *The Marshall Plan and Its Meaning.* Ithaca, N.Y.: Cornell University Press, 1955.

Price, Matthew C. *The Advancement of Liberty.* Westport, Conn.: Greenwood, 2008.

Schlesinger, Arthur M. Jr. *A Life in the Twentieth Century.* New York: Houghton Mifflin, 2000.

Sorel, Eliot, and Pier Carlo Padoan, eds. *The Marshall Plan: Lessons Learned for the 21st Century.* Paris: OECD, 2008.

Taft, Robert. "Text of Taft Speech Here Listing Objections to Scale of Marshall Plan for Aid To Europe." *New York Times,* November 11, 1947, pp. 20–21.

Treaty of Maastricht. Available online. URL: http://eur-lex. europa.eu/en/treaties/dat/11992M/htm/11992M.html.

Vandenberg, Arthur. *The Private Papers of Senator Vandenberg.* Westport, Conn.: Greenwood Press, 1974.

White, Theodore H. *Fire in the Ashes.* New York: Sloane, 1968.

FURTHER RESOURCES

BOOKS

Anderson, Janet. *The Senate*. New York: Chelsea House, 2007.

Bergan, Michael. *The Berlin Airlift*. Minneapolis: Compass Point, 2007.

Brager, Bruce L. *The Iron Curtain: The Cold War in Europe*. New York: Chelsea House, 2004.

Foley, Michael. *Harry S. Truman*. New York: Chelsea House, 2003.

Gottfried, Ted. *The Cold War*. Brookfield, Conn.: Twenty-First Century Books, 2003.

Isserman, Maurice. *The Korean War*. New York: Facts On File, 2003.

———. *World War II*. New York: Facts On File, 2003.

Kahn, Peggy. *The European Union*. New York: Chelsea House, 2008.

Lubetkin, Wendy. *George Marshall*. New York: Chelsea House, 1989.

Schantz, Sonja, and Gerry Donaldson. *Germany*. New York: Chelsea House, 2004.

Schleppler, Bill. *How a Law Is Passed*. New York: Chelsea House, 2007.

Zuehlke, Jeffrey. *Joseph Stalin*. Minneapolis: Lerner, 2006.

WEB SITES

British Broadcasting Corporation's Cold War content
http://www.bbc.co.uk/history/worldwars/coldwar/

The European Union
  http://europa.eu/index_en.htm

The George C. Marshall Foundation
  http://www.marshallfoundation.org/index.html

George Marshall's Harvard Speech
  http://www.oecd.org/document/10/0,3746,en_2649_
    201185_1876938_1_1_1_1,00.html

The German Marshall Fund
  http://www.gmfus.org

Harry S. Truman Library and Museum
  http://www.trumanlibrary.org/whistlestop/study_
    collections/marshall/large/

The Library of Congress, "For European Recovery:
  The Fiftieth Anniversary of the Marshall Plan"
  http://www.loc.gov/exhibits/marshall/marsintr.html

The National Archives' Marshall Plan content
  http://www.archives.gov/research/alic/reference/military/
    cold-war-and-marshall-plan.html

Selling Democracy: Films of the Marshall Plan, 1948–1953
  http://www.sellingdemocracy.org/

PICTURE CREDITS

INDEX

38th parallel
  fighting along, 73-75
  stalemate at, 72

A

Acheson, Dean, 81
Adenauer, Konrad, 90-91
Afghanistan, 53
Africa, 98
Albania, 27, 30
Allied nations, 80
  bombing campaigns, 9, 62
  countries, 9, 33, 47, 52, 54-55,
    90
  troops, 10, 14, 32
  victory, 7
American Association for the
  United Nations, 25
Asia, 9, 73, 98
Atlantic Ocean, 19, 35, 49, 59, 64
Attlee, Clement, 92
Australia, 74
Austria, 30, 90, 96
  aid to, 49
Axis nations
  countries, 9

B

ballistic missiles, 9
BBC. *See* British Broadcasting
  Corporation
Belgium, 9, 30, 78, 94, 97
Berlin, 90
  airlift, 54-56
  Blockade, 52, 54-56
  wall, 52, 99
Bevin, Ernest
  government, 19-20, 25, 27, 31,
    77

Bidault, Georges
  government, 20, 25, 27
Bissell, Richard
  and the ECA, 48-49, 70, 78, 81
Bradley, Omar, 14
British Broadcasting Corporation
  (BBC), 19-20
Brussels, 99
Bulgaria, 27, 30, 62, 96

C

Callender, Harold, 23
Canada, 74, 97
capitalism, 13
CED. *See* Committee for
  Economic Development
CEEC. *See* Committee of Euro-
  pean Economic Cooperation
China, 9, 45, 72-73
  military, 75
Chinese Civil War, 73
Churchill, Winston, 7, 12, 15, 93
Clay, Lucius, 54
Clayton, Will, 23, 41
Cold War, 52-53, 71-72, 86, 91,
  96-97
Cominform. *See* Communist
  Information Bureau
Committee for Economic
  Development (CED), 47
Committee for the Marshall
  Plan, 64
Committee of European
  Economic Cooperation
  (CEEC), 31-32
Communism
  in Europe, 13, 21, 37, 40-41,
    45, 51-54, 76, 80, 87, 89
  fight against, 51-54, 73, 98

ABOUT THE AUTHOR

G.S. PRENTZAS is the author of more than 20 books for young readers. He wrote *The World Health Organization* in Chelsea House's GLOBAL ORGANIZATIONS series and *Gideon v. Wainwright* in Chelsea House's GREAT SUPREME COURT DECISIONS series. He lives near New York City.

The author dedicates this book to the memory of his uncle, Jack Flowers, a veteran of World War II.